TEACHER'S
EVERY DAY COUNTS®
CALENDAR MATH

Janet G. Gillespie

•

Patsy F. Kanter

GRADE
1

GReaT SouRce®
EDUCATION GROUP

A Houghton Mifflin Company
Wilmington, Massachusetts

Acknowledgments

We offer special thanks to

- **our colleagues and mentors:** Beth Ardell, Brenda Bartell, Jacquelyn Brown, Leigh Eisen, Christine Emery, Beth Gagnon, Bette Johnsrud, Sonya Kelley, Mary Laughlin, Rolia Manyongai, Carolyn Morris, Lori Oman, Veronica Paracchini, Charlotte Stolberg, Pam Wallace, Mary Weber, JoAnn Wiser, and Nada Wood for their work with children and helpful insight. Also, the late Mary Baratta-Lorton, Donna Burk, Marilyn Burns, Constance Kamii, Kathy Richardson, Allyn Snider, and the late Robert Wirtz for inspiring and guiding our work in the classroom through their workshops and writing.
- **our principals:** Sharon Nelson, Dot Brown, and Linda Harris for their leadership.
- **our families:** Tim, Nathan, and Josh Gillespie; and David, Julie, and Nathan Kanter for their support and patience.
- **our mothers:** the late Louise H. Friedler and Anna Giske for introducing us to the fun of math and games at an early age.
- **the Great Source team:** Rick Duthe, Sandra Easton, Susan Rogalski, and Richard Spencer for making this book a reality.

Credits

Cover Design: Dinardo Design
Cover Illustration: Rob Dunlavey
Electronic Art: PC&F, Inc.

Copyright © 1998 by Great Source Education Group, Inc. All rights reserved.

Permission to reproduce the Teaching Resources pages is granted to the users of *Every Day Counts Calendar Math*. No other part of this work may be reproduced or transmitted in any form or by any means, electronic or mechanical, including photocopying and recording, or by any information storage or retrieval system without the prior written permission of Great Source Education Group, Inc., unless such copying is expressly permitted by federal copyright law. Address inquiries to Permissions, Great Source Education Group, Inc., 181 Ballardvale Street, Wilmington, MA 01887.

Printed in the United States of America

Great Source and *Every Day Counts* are registered trademarks of Houghton Mifflin Company

International Standard Book Number: 0-669-44097-3

4 5 6 7 8 9 10 11 12 VCG 02 01 00 99 98

URL address: http://www.greatsource.com/

EVERY DAY COUNTS

CALENDAR MATH

 WHAT IS *EVERY DAY COUNTS*® *CALENDAR MATH*?

 AN INTERACTIVE MATH BULLETIN BOARD

Every Day Counts Calendar Math provides 10 to 15 minutes of supplementary math instruction each day. It revolves around a simple bulletin board containing a Calendar, a Counting Tape to count the days of school, and other elements that change throughout the year, such as Clocks, Coin Counters, and Graphs. Each day students and their teachers use current data from the various elements on the bulletin board to get a new angle on mathematical relationships. It's almost like looking through a kaleidoscope, with every turn bringing a new array of relationships to examine. While discussing the data from the bulletin board for a few minutes a day, students at every grade level get the opportunity to analyze data, perceive patterns, explore mathematical relationships, and communicate their thinking.

Calendar Math was strongly influenced by the ideas of Donna Burk, Allyn Snider, Paula Symonds, the late Mary Baratta-Lorton, and the late Robert Wirtz. The Calendar ideas, gathered from the work of Baratta-Lorton, Burk, Snider, and Symonds, convinced us that daily examination of mathematical relationships could help children of all grade levels build mathematical

competence and confidence. Robert Wirtz's strong belief that children could learn from sharing their discoveries encouraged us to make students' observations and thinking the driving force behind our activities.

We began developing different activities involving a high level of student interaction that could be incorporated daily. Therefore, *Calendar Math* provides different elements for each grade level, during each month of the school year. These elements focus on mathematical relationships central to the curriculum at each grade. As a result, kindergartners to sixth graders are offered daily exposure to place value, measurement, time, money, mental math, geometry, estimation, patterns and functions, graphing, and statistics. This exposure is visual, hands-on, and interactive.

 WHY USE *EVERY DAY COUNTS* *CALENDAR MATH*?

 A LITTLE TIME = A LOT OF MATH

Our experience with elementary students has taught us that constructing mathematical understandings takes time—often more than a unit of study can provide. With *Calendar Math*, students have the entire year to explore critical concepts at their grade level through multiple experiences. For example, in the primary grades, developing an understanding of how our base ten system works is critical. To support this, the Daily Depositor and Counting Tape provide concrete experiences with grouping, counting, and recording hundreds, tens, and ones. In grade 5, students are guided through a difficult transition by investigating increments with the Fraction A Day and Daily Decimal elements. These important concepts are presented over an extended time rather than in one unit, providing the opportunity to preview as well as review them throughout the year.

Q HOW IS *EVERY DAY COUNTS CALENDAR MATH* SPECIAL?

A CLASSROOM DISCUSSION: THE HEART OF *EVERY DAY COUNTS CALENDAR MATH*

Calendar Math gives students the opportunity to talk about what they see and to understand and learn from one another. Many sample questions provide a springboard for classroom discussion. The purpose of asking so many questions is to encourage children's thinking. Asking students to share the various ways they arrived at answers helps them see that there are many ways to work with numbers and to approach problems. They also see that the same way of working out a problem may be explained in several different ways. Class discussions are rich in communication and language when students share their thinking and learn from one another.

Q HOW IS *EVERY DAY COUNTS CALENDAR MATH* ORGANIZED?

A BY GRADE LEVEL, BY MONTHS

Each grade level book is organized by month. On the opening page for each month, there is a picture of what the elements on the Every Day Bulletin Board might look like at some point during the month. A brief overview of suggested elements and activities for the month follows. When each element is introduced, you will find the **FOCUS** for that activity, a list of **MATERIALS,** an explanation of how to conduct an **UPDATE PROCEDURE** daily, and suggestions for encouraging **DISCUSSION** throughout the month. These discussions invite students to analyze the accumulating data, make predictions, and justify their thinking. Sometimes there are **HELPFUL HINTS** for preparing or enhancing an activity. These have often originated from teachers using the elements of *Calendar Math* in their classrooms.

Q *EVERY DAY COUNTS CALENDAR MATH* HAS SO MANY ACTIVITIES. HOW CAN I CHOOSE?

A START SMALL AND ADD ON LATER

Skim the introduction to each month and thumb through the book to see the range of elements that make up *Calendar Math* at your grade level. The first year we suggest you start small and limit the number of elements you share with the class. Your preparation can be minimized, and your primary focus can be on facilitating students' discussion. We have found that less is often more when getting started with these new activities.

You might begin with the yearlong elements—the Counting Tape and Calendar. Or you might choose an element that provides experience with a topic students have had difficulty with in the past. Or you might simply pick elements that are most interesting to you. Your interest will most likely have a positive effect on your students' involvement.

HOW DO I GET THE MATERIALS FOR *EVERY DAY COUNTS CALENDAR MATH*?

 PURCHASE THE KIT

Materials for *Calendar Math* are available in a kit. There is a section in the back of the Teacher's Guide with Teaching Resources copymasters to be used to accompany the elements. Photocopying and using clear pockets or lamination on these copymasters will allow for daily updating by using colored markers. Small vinyl pockets or photo album pockets can function as clear pockets, to hold money or objects. Keeping a small supply box with pushpins and markers near your Calendar is very handy. The elements used throughout *Calendar Math* are the Calendar and the Counting Tape. Elements featured during the year in Grade 1 include the Clock, Coin Counter, and Daily Depositor. Below are explanations for using each of these elements:

CALENDAR: Use the Every Day Calendar and Month Strips provided in the kit. Make a $\frac{3}{4}$-inch horizontal cut at the top of each square on the Calendar. This way the Calendar Pieces can be attached to the Calendar with paper clips. When placing patterns on the calendar, use the numbered Calendar Pieces provided in the kit or create Calendar Pieces with the Teaching Resources copymasters in the back of the book. Feel free to use your own cutouts to form a different pattern each month.

COUNTING TAPE: Use the adding machine tape provided in the kit. This is used to record the number of days students come to school. Many teachers use 3-inch squares of construction paper or self-stick removable notes to form the patterns on the Counting Tape. Some commercially-made pads of paper have an adhesive backing and are available in a variety of colors, making the Counting Tape more visually attractive for the students.

CLOCK: Use the Every Day Clock cardstock and the clock hands included in the kit. The Clock should be inserted into a 9" × 12" vinyl pocket and the hands attached to the outside of the pocket. Cut out clock hands from the cardstock to begin with and store the rest. Many copies of the hands

have been provided since they will probably need to be replaced during the year. You can also copy the Every Day Clock copymaster in the back of this book and laminate it so it can be updated easily every day. In either case, use a marker with erasable ink whenever you update the Clock. The Every Day Clock also provides students with the added benefit of seeing the time written in digital notation. If you have access to a geared demonstration clock, plan to use it along with the Every Day Clock.

COIN COUNTER: Use the clear pockets provided in the kit, or use your own acetate pockets such as those used in photograph albums, to act as money holders for coins. Use copies of the Every Day Graph copymaster in the back of this book or blank sheets of paper to record the total amount of the day's combinations of coins.

DAILY DEPOSITOR: You will need two sheets of $8\frac{1}{2} \times 14$" construction paper to create the background for the Depositor, one light-colored sheet for the ones place and a dark-colored sheet for the tens place. The clear pockets are provided in the kit. During the year, collections of pennies, buttons, rocks, shells, and canceled postage stamps will be used to help children create number comparison stories and to provide exposure to place value.

 HOW DO I GET STARTED WITH *EVERY DAY COUNTS CALENDAR MATH*?

 CREATE THE *EVERY DAY COUNTS CALENDAR MATH* BULLETIN BOARD IN A HIGHLY VISIBLE AREA OF YOUR ROOM

First, you will need to choose a place in your room where you can create a bulletin board that is easily accessible to you and your students. Many teachers who use *Calendar Math* do not hang everything in one location. Sometimes graphs are placed across the room or the Counting Tape is hung under the chalkboard. What really counts is that you and your students can see and interact easily at the bulletin board. Then, decide which elements you want to begin with and have those pieces ready for the first day of school or as soon thereafter as possible.

EVERY DAY COUNTS

CALENDAR MATH

TABLE OF CONTENTS

GRADE 1

Measurement: estimating and measuring length using nonstandard and standard units; comparing the lengths of common objects

Graph: collecting weather data; comparing and interpreting data on three picture graphs

Counting Tape: extending number patterns above one hundred and using mental math; understanding place value

Totally Ten Count: grouping and counting by hundreds, tens, and ones; adding or subtracting 10 and 100 using place value models

Calendar: analyzing and predicting patterns; recognizing various two-dimensional shapes; exploring symmetry

Birthday Data: reading, comparing, and ordering numbers to 31; solving problems and using mental math

Coin Counter: solving problems with coins; figuring change by counting up

Daily Domino: working with combinations to 10; seeing part and whole relationships; counting up to find a difference

Measurement: estimating and comparing capacity and weight using nonstandard units

Graph: collecting and recording data on a graph; recognizing two- and three-dimensional shapes in the environment

GETTING STARTED

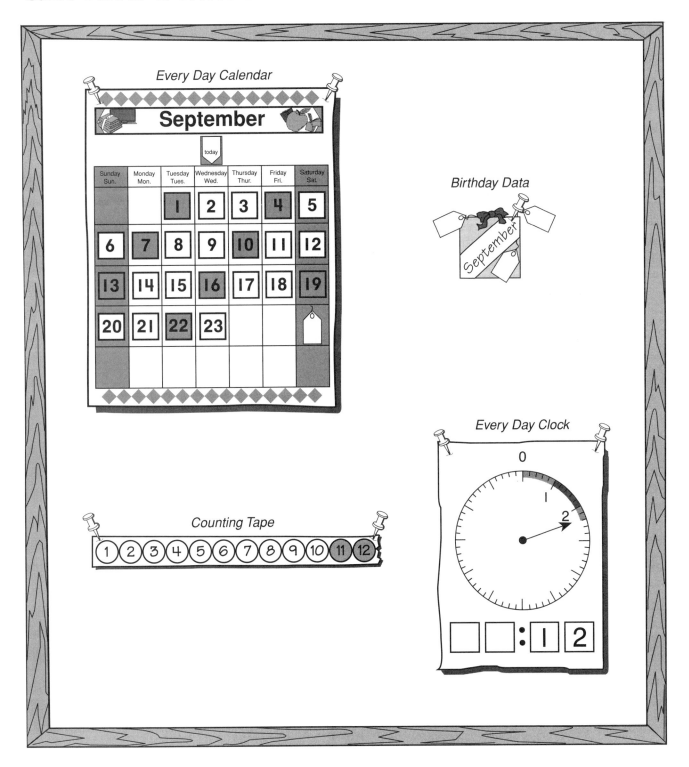

Every Day Calendar

September

today

Sunday Sun.	Monday Mon.	Tuesday Tues.	Wednesday Wed.	Thursday Thur.	Friday Fri.	Saturday Sat.
		1	2	3	4	5
6	7	8	9	10	11	12
13	14	15	16	17	18	19
20	21	22	23			

Birthday Data

September

Counting Tape

1 2 3 4 5 6 7 8 9 10 11 12

Every Day Clock

0

1

2

☐ ☐ : 1 2

Getting started requires only a few elements of Every Day Counts Calendar Math during the time that establishing classroom routines and getting to know the children are your highest priorities. The elements for September include the Counting Tape, Clock, Calendar, and Birthday Data. The first two elements make use of the days of school, so there is an advantage to beginning them early. The Counting Tape should be displayed by the first day of school.

EVERY DAY ELEMENT   COUNTING TAPE

FOCUS
▶ Developing number sense
▶ Counting with one-to-one correspondence
▶ Grouping and counting by 10's and 1's
▶ Understanding place value
▶ Matching quantities with numerals
▶ Comparing and ordering quantities
▶ Counting on and counting back
▶ Developing number patterns and a sense for mental math
▶ Experiencing duration
▶ Solving problems

MATERIALS
Adding-machine tape, 200 circle cutouts with 3-inch diameters (20 each of 10 different colors), 20 yellow $\frac{3}{4}$-inch dot stickers

OVERVIEW
The Counting Tape is a time line for recording each day of first grade. As children see a new circle added to the Counting Tape each day and see the number for that school day recorded, they will become more familiar with increasing quantities and the numbers that represent them.

Every 10 days the color of the circles changes, helping children to see the patterns from decade to decade. As they count the shapes each day, they practice the counting sequence. They also count the groups of 10 and the ones to develop an understanding of place value. From the 101st day on, children see the pattern of the first 99 days repeated.

When asked questions such as, "What day of school will it be in 5 more school days?" children develop language that describes the passage of time and gain skills in counting on.

The Counting Tape reveals other relationships as well. Its linearity assists children in making comparisons. For example, they can see that a row of 20 is twice as long as a row of 10 or that 16 is 6 more circles than 10 and 4 fewer than 20. It is easy to see which is more, 12 or 21. Making many such comparisons fosters children's development of number sense.

FREQUENCY

Update and discuss daily.

UPDATE PROCEDURE

Attach one circle to the Counting Tape each school day beginning with the first day of school. Use circles that are all the same color for the first 10 days, then use a different color for the next 10, and so on for each decade to 100. The color change with each 10 days transforms the Counting Tape into a place-value model, showing a new display of tens and ones every day. Ask the class to count by 1's to the day's number. Then count by 10's and 1's, clapping on the last multiple of 10 as a reminder for everyone to begin counting by 1's. For example, on the 16th day of school, children count "10 (with a clap), 11, 12, 13, 14, 15, 16."

After counting the circles, record the number for the present day on the day's circle.

DISCUSSION FOR THE FIRST DAY

As soon as possible, introduce the Counting Tape. Explain to children that each circle on the counting tape is for each day they come to school this year. Ask them to call out the number for you to write on each circle, beginning with 1 for Day 1. You might ask them how far around the room they think the Counting Tape will stretch by the 100th day of school. They will consider this question several times in the months ahead, so have them record their thoughts for reference.

DISCUSSION LATER IN THE MONTH

Once or twice a week, in addition to the counting and recording activities, engage children in considering other questions. These questions can encourage children to see many relationships and help them construct a variety of number concepts. Below are some sample questions that might be asked on Day 16, for example. The list of possibilities is long in order to provide a broad range of questions that can be adapted for use on any school day.

Some questions to develop number sense and vocabulary for comparing:

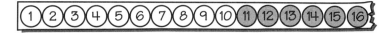

▶ Which is more, 16 circles or 13 circles?
▶ What will the next number be? The next 3 numbers?
▶ What number came before today's number?
▶ What day of school came just after Day 6?
▶ What day of school came just before Day 12?
▶ What day of school came between Day 3 and Day 5?
▶ What day of school came just after Day 7 and just before Day 9?

Some questions to foster understanding of place value:
▶ How many groups of ten do we have so far? How many extras?
▶ How many circles would we have if we took off a group of ten?
▶ How many circles would we have if we added a group of ten?

Some questions to encourage counting on and counting back:
▶ What day of school will it be in 3 more days?
▶ What day of school was it 2 school days ago?
▶ How many more days must we come to school to reach the 18th day?
▶ How many days have we come to school since the 12th day?

Some questions to encourage sorting and the search for patterns:
▶ How many more days until the color will change? How do you know?
▶ How are the circles that come after 10 different from the first 10?
▶ How are the circles that come after 10 like the first 10 circles?
▶ Can we find a pattern that starts with the first 10 circles and then repeats in the circles that follow?

The purpose of asking such questions is to foster children's thinking. Understanding how children arrive at their answers—the processes and strategies they use—is more important than the correct or incorrect responses they may give. By frequently asking, "Would you like to share *how* you got your answer?" we help children focus their thinking.

In the beginning of first grade, only a few children may choose to try to explain how they solved a problem. But as children experience similar questions posed throughout the year, more will develop the confidence to share their strategies. Occasionally, when no one has words to describe a strategy or when no one wants to share, you may want to describe your method. Then ask if anyone solved it a different way.

HELPFUL HINTS
▶ Adding a yellow dot sticker to the center of the zero in the numerals 10, 20, 30, and so on, helps to make the tens stand out. Some teachers draw on a face and name zero "Zero the Hero." Children begin to anticipate its appearance every few weeks.

▶ If cutting out circles seems too time consuming, substitute 3-inch squares cut on the paper cutter. Squares work best as discrete shapes for counting when turned on their ends to resemble diamonds.

▶ If you have parent volunteers or older students to help with preparation, you might want to consider the special appeal of animal or object cutouts, for example, cutouts of a school-house or school bus (TR22). One teacher, Linda Anderson of New Orleans, lined up turtles around her first grade class-room one year. On the 100th day, the 100th turtle became a true standout when the children decorated its shell with 100 sequin "jewels."

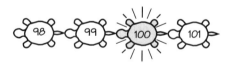

▶ If your school year begins in August, begin using the Counting Tape the first week.

EVERY DAY ELEMENT

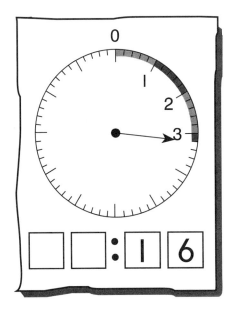

FOCUS
- ▶ Experiencing duration
- ▶ Understanding analog and digital clocks
- ▶ Learning how many minutes in an hour
- ▶ Counting by 5's and 1's
- ▶ Reading the minute hand

MATERIALS
Every Day Clock cardstock or a copy of the Every Day Clock (TR8) with minute hand attached; 9" × 12" clear pocket; green and red markers with erasable ink

OVERVIEW
For the first 60 days of school, the Every Day Clock will have only a minute hand, which moves forward one minute per school day. Thus children get daily experience counting the minutes by 5's and 1's and reading the minute hand. Once January comes, the routine changes; an hour hand is added. Both hour and minute hands will move to show an hour passing for each day of the month. Beginning in March, hour and minute hands are considered together.

Throughout the year, the digital notation is used to help children gain confidence in reading both kinds of clocks. Periodic duration experiments give children the chance to estimate and experience how long a second or a minute is.

FREQUENCY
Update daily and discuss two or three times a week.

UPDATE PROCEDURE
Beginning with the first day of school, move the minute hand on the Every Day Clock ahead one minute each school day. At the same time, color in one red space along the circumference of the clock face. On the fifth day of school, write a 1 just inside the first 5-minute mark to represent one group of 5. On the 6th through the 10th day of school, color in each minute space using a second color, such as green. Using alternating colors for each five-minute group helps children count and group by fives and ones. On the 10th day of school, write a 2 for two groups of 5, and on the 15th day, a 3 for three groups of 5, and so on.

Each day read the position of the minute hand, counting by 1's first. Using the Every Day Clock, go back and count again by 5's and 1's, clapping on the last 5 to signal the change to counting by 1's. Finally, record the minutes shown by the minute hand, using the digital clock below the clock face. This number should agree with the Counting Tape, which also reflects the days of school.

SAMPLE DISCUSSION FOR THE FIRST DAY

Teacher: (Showing the Every Day Clock to the class) Look around the room. Can you find something that looks a little like this picture?

Child: The clock.

Teacher: Yes, this picture is a lot like our clock. It is round and it has the same marks going around the edge. How is this picture different from the classroom clock?

Child: The picture doesn't have any numbers on it.

Child: The picture just has one hand on it. Our clock has two hands.

Teacher: Good observations. Look at the classroom clock right now. The short hour hand tells us it is just a little after 9:00. The long minute hand pointed straight up when it was 9:00, but now it has moved to the 10th tiny minute mark, so the time is 9:10 or 10 minutes after 9. To help us learn how to read the minute hand, we're going to move the long minute hand on our Bulletin Board clock *ahead* one minute each day we come to school. If we begin straight up at zero and today is the first day of school, which minute mark shall we point it toward today?

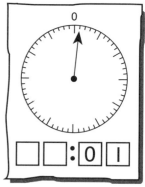

1st day of school

11:19

Classroom Clock

19th day of school

DISCUSSION LATER IN THE MONTH

At least twice a week, after counting the minutes, talk about how many groups of five have passed. Ask children to predict how they will read the minute hand when it reaches the next 5-minute mark. How many more days will it take to get there?

You might designate some days for noticing when the minute hand on the classroom clock matches the position of the minute hand on the Every Day Clock. Children can raise their hands when they notice these special times during the day. Take a moment to read the classroom clock, helping children read the hour hand first and then having them read the minutes.

HELPFUL HINTS

▶ The digital notation of minutes can be wiped off and rewritten each day. Some teachers prefer to replace this record with pockets holding number cards. The digits can be changed each day to tell the time shown on the Every Day Clock.

▶ With the emphasis on minutes and reading minutes past the hour on the Clock, it would be helpful for children to have a sense of how long one minute is. Ask them to rest their heads on their arms and observe one minute of quiet.

▶ We have chosen to use the terms *long* and *short* instead of *big* and *little* when referring to the minute and hour hands.

▶ Bringing in a digital clock may speed up some children's clock-reading skills since they can compare the digits to the positions of the hands on the classroom clock. At home, both types of clocks are rarely in the same room, making such comparisons difficult.

▶ Although the Every Day Clock is used through December to emphasize the minute hand, it is suggested that the classroom clock or a geared demonstration clock be used simultaneously throughout these months as an aid in reading the hour and minutes together.

▶ If your school year begins in August, begin using the Clock the first week.

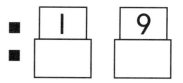

FOCUS
▶ Analyzing and predicting patterns
▶ Knowing the days of the week in order
▶ Counting with one-to-one correspondence
▶ Matching quantities with numerals
▶ Comparing numbers
▶ Developing number sense

Calendar Pieces

MATERIALS
Every Day Calendar, September Month Strip, September Calendar Pieces; or square shapes from Calendar Cutouts (TR21); Today Marker (TR21), Calendar Record (TR15), Date Cards (TR2) (optional)

SUGGESTED PATTERN FOR SEPTEMBER
The September Calendar Pieces use green and white squares to create an ABB pattern in the order green square, white square, white square. If you choose to use the squares from the Calendar Cutouts (TR21), you can use the same or any other color pair to create the pattern. Write the dates on the pieces before posting.

OVERVIEW
The Every Day Calendar uses numbered Calendar Pieces that create a specific color pattern as they are attached during the course of the month. Because the Calendar Pieces gradually reveal a pattern, the Calendar provides an invitation to search for connections between the color and number patterns that appear. "What will be the color of today's date?" encourages children to think. They consider all the accumulated data as they search for a repeating pattern. Early predictions, based on too little data, may be incorrect, which will allow children to see how easy it is to jump to conclusions. As more of the pattern is revealed, children can determine the color of a piece that will appear on any future date using a variety of strategies. At month's end, ask children to describe all the different patterns they see.

FREQUENCY
Update daily. On Monday, add the Calendar Pieces for Saturday and Sunday. Once a week allow for an extended discussion of the patterns.

UPDATE PROCEDURE
Display the name of the month above the Calendar and help children read it aloud. On the first day of the month, attach the Calendar Piece (numbered 1) for that day. (If the month begins on a day without school, catch up to the current date.) Each day, as you attach the new Calendar Piece, help the class read the date using the Calendar. For example, "Today is Tuesday, September 8." Attach the Today Marker above the day's name to indicate the day of the week.

DISCUSSION FOR THE BEGINNING OF THE MONTH

Toward the end of the first week, you might ask some of the following questions to focus attention on the Calendar:

▶ What numbers have we seen so far?

▶ Would someone like to point out tomorrow's space on the Calendar?

▶ What number do you think will be on tomorrow's piece?

▶ How are the pieces we've put up so far the same? (All are squares and all have numbers.)

▶ How are they different? (The colors change and the numbers are different.)

If some children recognize the possibility of a repeating color pattern at this time, acknowledge the patterns they point out and suggest it will be fun to see if the colors continue in this way. If no mention of a pattern is made, do not point it out at this time.

SAMPLE DISCUSSION FOR THE END OF THE SECOND WEEK

Teacher: Let's look at the Calendar. Today is September 11th. What will tomorrow be?

Class: The 12th.

Teacher: Yes. What color do you think tomorrow's piece will be?

Child: White.

Teacher: Who agrees and thinks it will be white? Who thinks it might be a different color? Would someone who thinks it will be white share how you decided that it will be white?

Child: There are 2 whites together all the time.

Teacher: Let's see. 2 and 3 are white; 5 and 6 are white; 8 and 9 are white. So you think that white 11 needs a white next to it? That makes sense. Would anyone else who thinks it will be white be willing to share another way you figured this out?

Child: The colors go green, white, white, green, white, white, so 12 is going to be white.

Teacher: Two children saw something happening over and over on the Calendar that helped them predict a color for 12. They each saw a pattern. One child saw the whites together over and over. Another saw the green, white, white pattern happen again and again. When you see a pattern happening over and over, it can often help you guess what will come next. Let's look at tomorrow's piece. Yes, it's white just as many of you predicted.

The activity might be extended to give children another way to experience patterns and their predictability. For example, translate the pattern into body movements. Encourage students to suggest a movement to go with green and another to go with white. Reading the pattern, "green, white, white" might translate to tap head, legs, legs with your hands. Instead of stopping on 11, continue to point to the blank spaces on the Calendar as children continue saying and acting out the pattern. Try it again doing something else on the greens and whites.

DISCUSSION LATER IN THE MONTH

Involve children in pattern activities once a week in September. At month's end, ask for volunteers to share the different patterns they see happening over and over on the Calendar. Suggestions for interpreting the calendar pattern in ways other than body movements will be made in upcoming months. By the year's end, children will be recognizing patterns all around them.

HELPFUL HINTS

▶ Some teachers prefer to make the Calendar Pieces go with the seasons, for example, red schoolhouses and yellow school buses (TR22) for September. These can add a special touch to the Calendar. Some seasonal calendar shapes are available commercially. Keep them simple so children can see the colors and numbers clearly.

▶ If you choose to use the Calendar Cutouts (TR21) to create your own Calendar Pieces, you may want to attach Date Cards (TR2) with paper clips instead of writing the date on the pieces. Then you can use the Calendar Pieces again in future years. Number the pieces before the first of the month. The Calendar Pieces can be kept out of sight in an envelope near the Calendar.

▶ When patterns appear in places in the environment other than the Calendar, point them out. Invite children to be on the lookout as well.

▶ While the Calendar Record (TR15) can be a useful tool for children to follow along at their desks, it also allows them to keep a record of the patterns that have developed throughout the school year. Some children may decide to follow up with Calendar Records of their own over summer vacation.

EVERY DAY ELEMENT

BIRTHDAY DATA

FOCUS

▶ Counting with one-to-one correspondence
▶ Reading, comparing, and ordering numbers to 30
▶ Solving problems and using mental math

MATERIALS

Birthday Package labeled with the name of the month (TR1), a Gift Tag (TR1) for each child who has a birthday this month labeled with the child's name and the date of birth

OVERVIEW

Displaying the month's birthday package with the gift tags attached guarantees that a child's birthday will not slip past without special recognition. The tags with the names and birthdays on them provide a fun focus for comparing numbers and determining how many days until each upcoming birthday.

FREQUENCY

Update monthly. Discuss at the beginning of the month and on each child's birthday.

UPDATE PROCEDURE

On the first day of school, have the month's birthday package with the attached tags placed near the Calendar. Sometime during the first week of school, invite children to help you read the names of the children whose tags are on the Package. The tags can be temporarily taken from the Package and used to mark the birthdays on the Calendar. After the child's birthday has passed, the tag can be re-attached to the month's Package.

DISCUSSION FOR THE BEGINNING OF THE MONTH

The tags on the Birthday Package offer experiences counting with one-to-one correspondence and ordering numbers. The following sample questions are intended to encourage this as children solve the problem of identifying the birthdays on this month's calendar.

- ▶ How many children have birthdays this month?
- ▶ What do you think the number on each tag means?
- ▶ If the number written on each tag is the birthday, which is the first birthday this month and whose is it?
- ▶ Whose birthday comes last this month?
- ▶ If we put the tags on the Calendar to mark each birthday, which space will get the first birthday of the month? Can you point to it? There is no number in that space, so how did you decide it should go there?
- ▶ Where will the next birthday be on the Calendar? Whose birthday is it?

Continue this process until all birthdays for the month have been identified on the Calendar.

DISCUSSION LATER IN THE MONTH

As the month goes along, you might occasionally ask children to determine how many days it will be until the next birthday. Then ask for volunteers to share how they got their answers. Some will count the spaces on the Calendar. Some will count on their fingers. Others may mentally compute a difference between the birthday and the present date.

With each passing birthday, if asked how many birthdays have come up so far in the month and how many are still to come, children have a chance to look at a different addition combination.

HELPFUL HINTS

- ▶ Opening a real birthday package would get a child's birthday off to a great start. It might contain cards from classmates and a special birthday crown, necklace, or badge, adorned with the child's name, to wear for the day.
- ▶ Many summer-birthday children experience disappointment when they are unable to celebrate their birthday with the class. It is, therefore, nice to choose an "unbirthday" for each of these children, perhaps six months before the real birthday on the same day of the month. (See December, page 39.)

OCTOBER

MOVING RIGHT ALONG

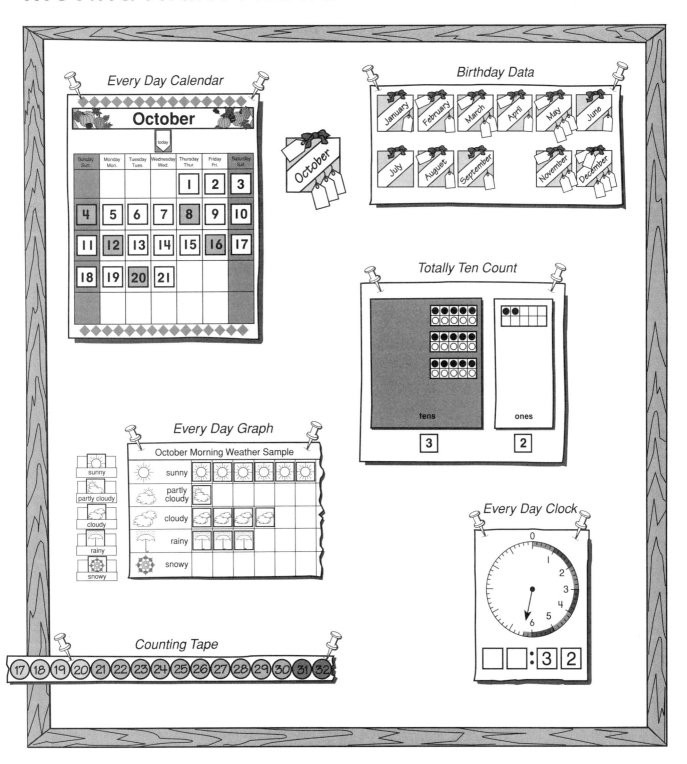

Every Day Calendar

October

today

Sunday Sun.	Monday Mon.	Tuesday Tues.	Wednesday Wed.	Thursday Thur.	Friday Fri.	Saturday Sat.
				1	2	3
4	5	6	7	8	9	10
11	12	13	14	15	16	17
18	19	20	21			

October

Birthday Data

January · February · March · April · May · June
July · August · September · November · December

Totally Ten Count

tens   ones
3   2

Every Day Graph

October Morning Weather Sample

sunny							
partly cloudy							
cloudy							
rainy							
snowy							

sunny
partly cloudy
cloudy
rainy
snowy

Every Day Clock

0 1 2 3 4 5 6

:3 2

Counting Tape

17 18 19 20 21 22 23 24 25 26 27 28 29 30 31 32

The Calendar Math elements that were introduced in September will be in use again. The Counting Tape and Clock will continue to reflect the numer of school days. The Calendar will present a new pattern. Birthday Data will display all the months' birthdays. The Totally Ten Count is a new element, which makes use of the number of school days to give children repeated experiences grouping in base ten. The other new element, the Every Day Graph, will display a sample of the season's autumn weather.

EVERY DAY ELEMENT   COUNTING TAPE

FOCUS
▶ Developing number sense
▶ Counting with one-to-one correspondence
▶ Grouping and counting by 10's and 1's
▶ Understanding place value
▶ Comparing and ordering quantities
▶ Counting on and counting back
▶ Developing number patterns and a sense for mental math
▶ Using the language of duration
▶ Solving problems

The MATERIALS, FREQUENCY, and UPDATE PROCEDURE for the Counting Tape continue from September. See pages 2 and 3 for a detailed description.

DISCUSSION DURING THE MONTH
Continue comparing, counting on, counting back, and counting by 10's and 1's, as you adapt many of the September questions to the larger numbers now appearing on the Counting Tape. Questions to develop number sense and the language of comparing on Day 25:
▶ Which came first, Day 13 or Day 15?
▶ What day of school came just after Day 3? Day 13? Day 23?
▶ What day of school came just before Day 5? Day 15? Day 25?
▶ What day came between Day 11 and Day 13?
▶ How many more is 25 than 20?

Questions to foster place value understanding:
▶ How many groups of ten do we have? How many extras?
▶ How many circles would we have if we took off the first group of ten?

Questions to encourage counting on and counting back:
▶ What day of school will it be in 3 more days?
▶ What day of school was 2 days ago?
▶ How many more days must we come to school to get up to the 29th day?

Questions that encourage sorting and the search for patterns:
► How many more days until the color will change again?
► How are the circles in the 20's like the circles up to 10?

Continue to ask children to share how they are arriving at their answers. Toward the end of the month, ask children to estimate how far they think the circles will stretch by the one hundredth day of school. If they made an earlier guess in September, ask them to compare it with their present estimates to see if they are the same or different.

HELPFUL HINTS
► On Days 20, 30, and 40, you might have the class decide on a new color for the next 10 circles. (No color should be used more than once until Day 101 when the color used for Days 1 to 10 reappears.)
► To help children relate the numbers on the Counting Tape to the numbers they see, hear, and use in their daily life in and out of school, play the game *Can You Catch Me, 11 to 20?* After Day 20, children are asked to be "scouts" on the lookout for the numbers 11 to 20 as they come up during the day at school and at home. When a child notices one of the targeted numbers in use at school, record the example on a large piece of construction paper the same color as the numbers 11–20 on the Counting Tape. Note the children's observations ("John has 16 crayons in his box," "There are 14 girls and 13 boys here today," and so on) with a few words, or a picture, or by attaching something to the construction paper. In the morning, add anecdotes and objects from home. Parents are often willing to support their child's growing awareness of numbers with this game at home, when invited to do so. Two weeks later, on Day 30, children can play *Can You Catch Me, 21 to 30?*

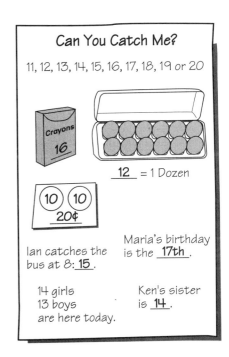

EVERY DAY ELEMENT

CLOCK

FOCUS
► Experiencing duration
► Understanding analog and digital clocks
► Learning how many minutes in an hour
► Counting by 5's and 1's
► Reading the minute hand

The MATERIALS, FREQUENCY, and UPDATE PROCEDURE for the Clock continue from September. See page 5 for a detailed description. Having a digital clock or a kitchen timer on hand will be helpful this month.

DISCUSSION DURING THE MONTH
Designate some days for catching the classroom clock when its minute hand matches the minutes on the Every Day Clock. Use the classroom clock to help children read the hour hand first and then the minutes.

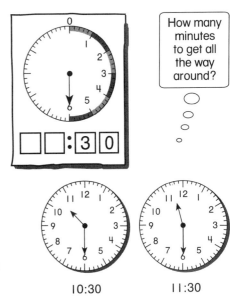

DISCUSSION FOR DAY 30

On the 30th day of school, when the minute hand has progressed to the 30-minute mark, point out that the hand is halfway around the Clock. Day 30 is also a good time to estimate how many minute marks are on the entire clock, if this has not yet come up. Encourage children to make some estimates and then count on together from minute mark 31 to 60 to find the exact number of minutes shown on the Every Day Clock.

HELPFUL HINTS

▶ To help children develop a sense of how long a half hour is, you might list a few television programs and regular school activities that are a half hour long.

▶ On Day 30, you might find setting a kitchen timer or digital alarm clock for the next 30-minute interval a helpful reminder to read the classroom clock.

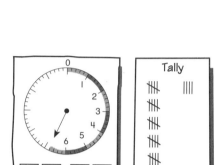

▶ You may wish to discuss the position of the hour hand when the minute hand is at the 30-minute mark.

▶ Some teachers record the days of school with tally marks by the Clock to show another way to count by 5's and 1's.

EVERY DAY ELEMENT   TOTALLY TEN COUNT

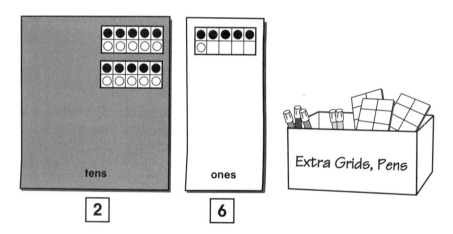

FOCUS

▶ Developing number sense
▶ Grouping and counting by 10's, 5's, and 1's
▶ Understanding place value
▶ Learning addition combinations for sums 5 through 10
▶ Adding or subtracting 10
▶ Developing a sense for mental math

MATERIALS

6" × 14" white paper for ones place, 14" × 14" dark construction paper for tens place, 20 Totally Ten Grids (TR7), a blue and a red felt pen or blue and red $\frac{3}{4}$" dot stickers (100 of each), 0–9 Digit Cards (TR4) on rings (optional)

OVERVIEW

The Totally Ten Count provides a pictorial representation of the number of school days. Every 10 days a Totally Ten Grid is filled and moved to the tens place. As children see the tens digit change each time this happens, they can gradually construct an understanding of our base ten numeration system. On the one hundredth day of school, they are exposed to the idea of 10 tens making 100. They learn to count by 100's, 10's, and 1's and to read and write numbers, knowing what the digits represent.

Another purpose of the Totally Ten Count is to provide repeated opportunities to see the combinations for the numbers 5 through 10 revealed in the dots within the Totally Ten Grid.

The Totally Ten Count also provides experience with counting by 10's and 1's, by 5's and 1's, and by 10's, 5's, and 1's. These skills are needed when reading a clock, adding coins, grouping and counting objects, and adding and subtracting numbers greater than 10.

FREQUENCY

Update daily and discusss two or more times a week.

UPDATE PROCEDURE

Update the Totally Ten Count to reflect the present day of school. (See Discussion for the First Day, below.) Every day of school from then on, place (or color) a dot on a Totally Ten Grid attached to the ones place. It will take 10 days to fill a grid. Five blue dots will accumulate across the top of a grid and then five red dots along the bottom. When a Totally Ten Grid becomes full, move it over to the tens place and attach a new, empty grid to the ones place. Each day record the number of tens and ones below each place. Have the class count by 10's and 1's and tell how many dots there are in all. On the 26th day of school, the class would count, "10, 20, 21, 22 . . . 26; 2 tens and 6 ones."

DISCUSSION FOR THE FIRST DAY

Begin by showing the children a Totally Ten Grid and asking them how many spaces they see. When they see how the Totally Ten Grid got its name, add one dot for each day the class has been in school so far. When a grid becomes full, move it to the tens place and begin adding dots to a new blank grid in the ones place. Have children say the total each time a dot is added and then say the number of full ten grids and ones. Stop on the present day of school.

You might begin, "Each day we come to school, we add a dot. How many dots do you think we will have put on our grids when we leave for summer vacation? Guess how many days you think we will be coming to first grade. I'll write your guesses on the chalkboard."

When children who wish to make a guess have each had a chance to do so, focus on the numbers on the chalkboard. Talk about the largest number and the smallest number. You might copy the numbers so you can compare these early guesses to ones the class will make later in the year.

DISCUSSION DURING THE MONTH

On the 30th day of school, ask children if they think the numeral 3 recorded under the tens place means 3 full ten grids or 3 dots. Review this idea other days during the month.

Some days focus discussion questions on the not-yet full grid on the ones side. When it holds 1 to 5 dots, you might ask, "How many more dots are needed to get to 5? How many to get to a full 10?" Children will come to know the combinations for 5 and 10 better with the filling of each grid.

HELPFUL HINTS

▶ Duplicate the Totally Ten Grids (TR7) and cut apart a year's supply of 20 grids. It is handy to put them along with the red and blue pens or dot stickers into an envelope near the Totally Ten Count display.

▶ The tens and ones record can be done in a variety of ways. Some teachers put up pads of paper and simply tear off the last day's record sheets to get a fresh place to write each day. Others put the record sheets in a clear pocket so they can be wiped off and written on with a transparency pen each day. Yet another way is to use a set of 0–9 Digit Cards (TR4) in pockets or on rings under each place. The cards are changed each day to show the new total on the Grids.

▶ Some teachers prefer to enlarge their Totally Ten Grids so that a variety of commercial stickers can be used.

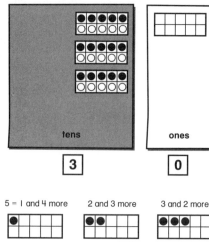

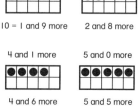

tear off paper | acetate record | digits on rings | digits in pockets

EVERY DAY ELEMENT

CALENDAR

FOCUS

▶ Recognizing, analyzing, and predicting patterns
▶ Knowing the days of the week in order
▶ Counting with one-to-one correspondence
▶ Counting on and counting back
▶ Matching quantities with numerals
▶ Solving problems

MATERIALS

Every Day Calendar, October Month Strip, October Calendar Pieces; or square shapes from Calendar Cutouts (TR21); Today Marker (TR21), Calendar Record (TR15)

SUGGESTED PATTERN FOR OCTOBER

The October Calendar Pieces use orange and red squares to create an AAAB pattern in the order orange square, orange square, orange square, red square. If you choose to use the squares from the Calendar Cutouts (TR21), you can use the same or any other color pair to create the pattern. Write the dates on the pieces before posting.

The FREQUENCY and UPDATE PROCEDURE continue from September. See page 7 for a detailed description. Once a week allow time for the children to share their observations and to interpret the month's pattern.

DISCUSSION AFTER THE SECOND WEEK

Reviewing the description of the September classroom discussion (see September, page 8) might be helpful at this time. Explain that a new pattern is beginning to appear on the October Calendar.

Some questions that tend to encourage observations and sharing might include:

▶   Today is Tuesday, October _____, so what will tomorrow be?
▶   What color do you think tomorrow's piece will be?
▶   Would someone who guessed this color volunteer to tell us how you figured this out? What helped you to know it would be this color?
▶   Could someone share a different way that helped them?
▶   Can someone else share another way you got the color?

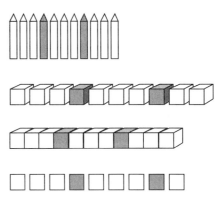

To help children broaden their concept of pattern beyond the Calendar, have them occasionally interpret the month's AAAB color pattern using body motions. For example, they might suggest stomping for orange and clapping for red. By letting the stomp, stomp, stomp, clap, stomp, stomp, stomp, clap, pattern continue on its own momentum after the Calendar Pieces run out, children can feel the strong predictability of pattern. Encourage children to suggest and try out two or three different interpretations of the pattern within a session. In addition to translating the pattern into body movements, involve children in creating pattern "trains" at least once during the month. The children can copy and extend the month's color pattern using materials available in the room. They will gain experience with making a pattern repeat as they line up construction paper pieces, colored blocks, connecting cubes, felt cutouts, or old crayons in the order of the month's color pattern. If children have had a lot of experience with patterning in kindergarten, they may be ready to choose their own colors to create an AAAB pattern with these materials.

DISCUSSION FOR THE END OF THE MONTH

To wrap up the month's discussion of patterns, ask children to communicate some of the things they have noticed about the Calendar this month. Some of their reponses may include:

▶   "The pattern was orange, orange, orange, red."
▶   "The reds go down like stairs."
▶   "There were more oranges than reds."
▶   "It goes 3 oranges and a red."
▶   "The orange ones go 1, 2, 3, skip, 5, 6, 7, skip, 9, 10, 11, skip . . . ."
▶   "The reds are 4, 8, 12, 16, 20, 24, 28."

You may want to write their observations on a large sheet of construction paper.

Helpful Hints

▶ Don't worry about those who aren't picking up the idea of pattern at this time. Month after month of experiencing patterns and listening to the observations of their "pattern-seeing" peers will help them. Ignore the stomps that should have been claps. By asking everyone to make predictions, but asking only for volunteers to share their reasoning, each child will begin to see patterns. The ranks of volunteers will expand with each passing week.

▶ Sometimes, when you are chanting the color pattern on the Calendar or doing body motions to the pattern, switch over to saying AAAB, AAAB while following the pattern. This may help some with seeing the pattern.

▶ For more on the significance of nurturing young children's awareness of pattern, and a plethora of meaningful ways of doing so, see *Mathematics Their Way* by Mary Baratta-Lorton, Addison-Wesley, 1976. *Developing Number Concepts* by Kathy Richardson, Addison-Wesley, 1984, and *Box It or Bag It Mathematics* by Donna Burk et al, Math Learning Center, 1988, also offer much in this area.

▶ You might have children keep a Calendar Record (TR15) of the pattern this month.

EVERY DAY ELEMENT   BIRTHDAY DATA

Focus

▶ Knowing the months of the year in order
▶ Counting, comparing, and ordering small quantities
▶ Counting with one-to-one correspondence to 31
▶ Reading, comparing, and ordering numbers to 31
▶ Solving problems and using mental math
▶ Interpreting organized data

Materials

12 Birthday Packages, each labeled with a different month (TR1); a Gift Tag (TR1) for each child, labeled with the child's name and date of birth

Overview

The Birthday Packages, arrayed somewhere in the classroom, provide a rich resource of organized numerical data of special interest to children. They will be happy to repeatedly consider questions which focus on the birthday information. Sequenced from January to December, the Packages help children learn the names and order of the months of the year. They also provide a fun focus for comparing numbers and doing mental math throughout the year.

FREQUENCY

Update and discuss at the beginning of each month. Follow up with several short discussions during the remaining weeks.

UPDATE PROCEDURE

At the beginning of each month, ask the class to point out the Birthday Package that matches the month written above the Calendar. Have the class name all the months in order, beginning this chant with the January Package. Then go through the sequence again, stopping with a clap on the present month. Mention those children who have birthdays this month, as indicated by the tags on the Package.

After looking at all the months together, you may take this month's package out of the lineup and feature it near the Calendar. The class can predict where each birthday will appear on the Calendar and mark it with the child's tag taken from the Birthday Package.

Suggestions on how to provide fair treatment to children with summer birthdays is addressed in September Helpful Hints. (See page 10.)

DISCUSSION FOR THE BEGINNING OF THE MONTH

Before you discuss the array of Birthday Packages, many children will have already found their names and noticed whether their package has only a few or many other tags. The following are examples of the kinds of questions that draw on children's observations and foster counting and comparing:

▶   How many names are on your birthday month's package?
▶   Which Birthday Package has the most names on it?
▶   Are there any months with no birthdays?
▶   Can you find a package with just one name on it?
▶   Can you find some packages with the same number of tags?
▶   Where is this month's October Birthday Package in the arrangement of all the months? If January is month one, and the next month, February, is month two, what month is October?

DISCUSSION DURING THE MONTH

Occasionally, ask children to find how many days until the next birthday. How much older is one October birthday child than another? Listen to those willing to share how they came to their conclusions. They may be using a variety of strategies from counting to mental math.

HELPFUL HINTS

▶   Try to display all the Packages as soon as possible so all children will feel included. When new children enter the classroom later in the year, be sure to add tags for them.
▶   Some teachers prefer to have children place their own tags on the Packages to kick off working with the class's birthday data. In this case, have a list of birthdays nearby for reference.

EVERY DAY ELEMENT   GRAPH

FOCUS
▶ Collecting and recording data on a graph over time
▶ Reading and interpreting data on a picture or bar graph
▶ Counting and comparing small quantities

MATERIALS
Every Day Graph (TR9), Weather Markers (TR12)

	October Morning Weather Sample					
sunny						
partly cloudy						
cloudy						
rainy						
snowy						

sunny
partly cloudy
cloudy
rainy
snowy

OVERVIEW
The Every Day Graph will offer a different opportunity each month for the class to gather, organize, and analyze quantitative data. The weather will be recorded with picture graphs in October, January, and April, providing a sample of each season's weather to compare. Results of probability experiments, student preference polls, and student predictions when estimating length, weight, or capacity will be graphed in other months. While the purpose of the Graph changes from month to month, each month's accumulating data provide frequent opportunities for counting and making comparisons. The Graph provides children with math they can see and talk about.

FREQUENCY
Update daily and discuss once a week.

UPDATE PROCEDURE
Each day have the class look outside and decide what the weather is like at that moment. Have a volunteer attach the appropriate weather symbol to the Graph. (It's best to make these observations at a similar time each day, since morning and afternoon weather patterns can vary a great deal in some locales.)

DISCUSSION FOR THE FIRST DAY
Instead of preparing the Weather Graph ahead of time, consider involving children in the problem-solving experience of setting it up. Tell children you have some pictures showing different kinds of weather. Ask them to guess what some of your pictures might be. Show them the Weather Markers and explain that they will use some of them to keep track of the weather on a graph this month and later in the winter and spring.

Have the class help decide which of the symbols are most appropriate for use in your region. Choosing just four or five conditions to monitor through the season will make the Graph easier for children to read and analyze. The common newspaper classifications of weather use only one symbol per day. *Cloudy* means cloudy conditions with no rain. If *windy* is suggested, discuss the problems this might pose when interpreting the data. For example, we cannot ask, "How many more windy than sunny days are there?" when some of the days that were windy may appear as sunny days on the Graph as well.

After determining the categories, help the class estimate how many squares are needed for each weather condition. Do we need one square for each school day in October? Is it possible in your area that it might be sunny every day or rainy every day? After the size of the Graph has been established, children can look for possible places in the room to display it. The space chosen may determine whether the data will need to be collected vertically or horizontally. Finally, children can decide how to label the rows or columns using the chosen weather symbols and place the first marker for the weather on the Graph.

DISCUSSION DURING THE MONTH

Once a week focus on the accumulating sample of October weather. To involve the class in counting and comparing, you might ask some questions similar to these:
▶ What kind of weather have we had most often?
▶ How many sunny days have we graphed so far this month?
▶ Is there any kind of weather we haven't seen on school days yet?
▶ Does our sample show more cloudy days or sunny days? How many more?
▶ How many school days would it need to rain for the rainy days to equal the cloudy days?
▶ How many days' weather are shown on the Graph?
▶ Does our Graph show all days in October to this day?

HELPFUL HINTS

▶ You may find it handy to store the Weather Markers in library pockets next to the Graph.
▶ Children can help color the symbols. Agree on the colors for the weather symbols beforehand so the categories will appear uniform. A variety of colors of clouds, for example, can detract from seeing the number of clouds in all.
▶ While the Weather Graph has been presented here as a picture graph, it could be done as a symbolic graph, if you prefer. Children can mark the Graph by pasting or pinning up colored paper squares, writing *x*'s, or shading in the squares with crayons. Plan on using the same format for the winter and spring Weather Graphs so the data from the different seasons can be easily compared.

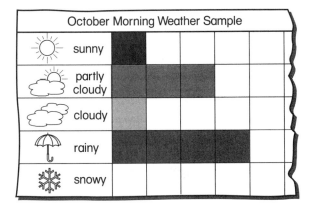

NOVEMBER

KEEPING UP THE MOMENTUM

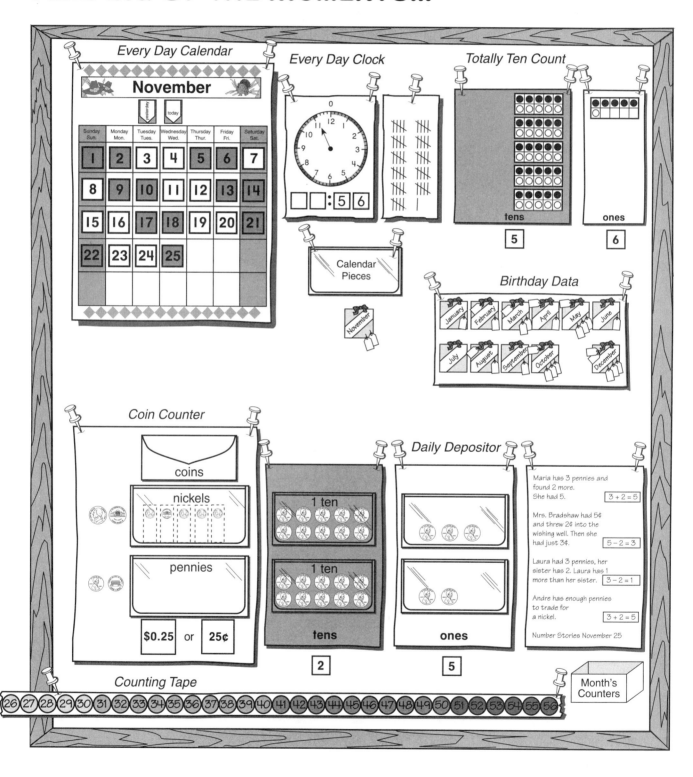

Every Day Calendar

November

Sunday Sun.	Monday Mon.	Tuesday Tues.	Wednesday Wed.	Thursday Thur.	Friday Fri.	Saturday Sat.
1	2	3	4	5	6	7
8	9	10	11	12	13	14
15	16	17	18	19	20	21
22	23	24	25			

Every Day Clock

: 5 6

Calendar Pieces

November

Totally Ten Count

tens 5

ones 6

Birthday Data

January February March April May June

July August September October November December

Coin Counter

coins

nickels

pennies

$0.25 or 25¢

1 ten

1 ten

tens 2

Daily Depositor

ones 5

Maria has 3 pennies and found 2 more. She had 5.   3 + 2 = 5

Mrs. Bradshaw had 5¢ and threw 2¢ into the wishing well. Then she had just 3¢.   5 − 2 = 3

Laura had 3 pennies, her sister has 2. Laura has 1 more than her sister.   3 − 2 = 1

Andre has enough pennies to trade for a nickel.   3 + 2 = 5

Number Stories November 25

Month's Counters

Counting Tape

26 27 28 29 30 31 32 33 34 35 36 37 38 39 40 41 42 43 44 45 46 47 48 49 50 51 52 53 54 55 56

In November, two new elements are added to Calendar Math. The Coin Counter introduces children to adding nickels and pennies. The Daily Depositor allows children to explore number combinations. The accompanying number stories provide exposure to symbolic number sentences. The Counting Tape, Clock, Totally Ten Count, and Birthday Data continue. The Calendar offers a new pattern. To allow more time for the new elements, a new Every Day Graph has not been included this month. Some classes will want to carry on with a November weather sample to compare with last month's.

EVERY DAY ELEMENT   COUNTING TAPE

FOCUS

▶ Developing number sense
▶ Counting with one-to-one correspondence
▶ Grouping and counting by 10's and 1's
▶ Understanding place value
▶ Comparing and ordering quantities
▶ Counting on and counting back
▶ Using number patterns and mental math
▶ Using the language of duration
▶ Solving problems

The MATERIALS, FREQUENCY, and UPDATE PROCEDURE for the Counting Tape continue from September. See pages 2 and 3 for a detailed description. Also included in the Materials this month is a Hundred Chart (TR16) or a meterstick.

DISCUSSION DURING THE MONTH

Continue to encourage comparing, counting on, counting back, and counting by 10's and 1's, as you adapt many of the September and October questions to the larger numbers appearing on the Counting Tape.

By the 40th day of school, children will have observed the counting sequence from 1 to 10 repeated 4 times. Here are some questions that help children see that they can use what they know about sets of 10 to work with higher numbers:

▶ Can you all find Day 4 on the Tape?
▶ What number did we put up 3 days after Day 4? Three days after Day 14? Three days after Day 24? Do you notice anything alike about all our answers? (They all have a 7.)
▶ Why are we always getting a 7? (4 and 3 more makes 7.)
▶ What day came one day before Day 8? One day before Day 18? One day before Day 28? One day before Day 38?
▶ Do you notice anything alike about all our answers? (They all have a 7 in them.)
▶ Why do we keep getting 7? (It always comes just before 8.)
▶ So what day will come up one day before we get to Day 58? Day 68?

DISCUSSION FOR DAY 50

Day 50 provides an appropriate occasion to explore the idea of 50 being halfway to 100. Since only the first 50 numbers are in view on the Tape, the class will need to look at another visual aid that shows the entire span from 1 to 100. The Hundred Chart or a meterstick will do. Coloring half the Chart will show 1 to 50 in the top half and 51 to 100 in the bottom half, helping children see 50 as half of 100. Counting centimeters by 10's to the end of the meterstick and then counting again to the mid-point will also show 50 to be halfway to 100. Then ask children to guess how far the Counting Tape will stretch by Day 100. Compare to the estimates they made last month.

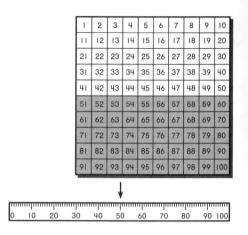

HELPFUL HINTS

▶ If the class has enjoyed the *Can You Catch Me?* activity in Helpful Hints (page 13), Day 50 is a good time to begin recording their observations of the numbers 41 to 50.

▶ On Day 50, have children color in the rows on the Hundred Chart (TR16) to 50, matching the colors of the decades on the Counting Tape. Coloring the Chart halfway is another way to see that 50 is half of 100. The Charts can be re-used 10, 20, or 50 days later to color in more rows of 10.

▶ Larger numbers present an excellent opportunity to let children explore with their calculators. After the Counting Tape discussion, let children verify their answers on the calculator.

EVERY DAY ELEMENT

CLOCK

FOCUS

▶ Experiencing duration
▶ Understanding analog and digital clocks
▶ Learning how many minutes in an hour
▶ Counting by 5's and 1's
▶ Reading the minute and hour hands

The MATERIALS, FREQUENCY, and UPDATE PROCEDURE for the Clock continue from September. See page 5 for a detailed description.

DISCUSSION DURING THE MONTH

Updating the Every Day Clock each day will give children practice reading the minute hand. However, to avoid the potential confusion when interpreting the hour hand, children will need many chances to read the classroom clock. Catching the minute hand on the classroom clock when it matches the one on the Every Day Clock, and then reading the hour and minutes together, will help. Ask the class to tell you how to show the hour hand on the Every Day Clock at these times. Gradually more children will notice that no matter how close the hour hand is to the next hour, it isn't that hour until the minute hand is straight up. Each day the class can figure out how many minutes until the hour by looking at the updated Every Day Clock.

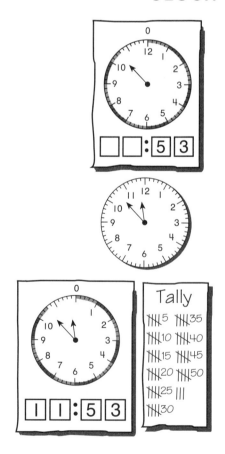

HELPFUL HINTS

▶ A geared demonstration clock can be used to show how the hour hand moves ever so slowly ahead just one hour each time the minute hand goes all the way around, ticking off 60 minutes.

▶ If your class reaches the 60th day of school in November, you might want to look ahead to the Clock Discussion for Day 60 in December on page 36.

EVERY DAY ELEMENT

FOCUS

▶ Developing number sense
▶ Grouping and counting by 10's, 5's, and 1's
▶ Understanding place value
▶ Learning addition combinations for sums 5 through 10
▶ Adding or subtracting 10
▶ Using mental math

TOTALLY TEN COUNT

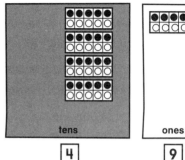

The MATERIALS and FREQUENCY for the Totally Ten Count continue from October. See pages 14 and 15 for a detailed description.

UPDATE PROCEDURE

Continue to add a new dot each school day to the Totally Ten Grid attached to the ones place. Continue moving the Grids to the tens place when they become full. Have the class count by 10's and 1's and tell how to record the tens and ones digits.

This month, in addition to the daily tens and ones count, try counting the total by 10's, 5's, and 1's. For example, on the 49th day of school the class would count, "10, 20, 30, 40, 45, 46, 47, 48, 49."

DISCUSSION DURING THE MONTH

When the Grid on the ones side holds from one to five dots, continue asking the class to consider how many more are needed to make 5 and how many are needed to make a full 10. This will provide frequent experience seeing the addition combinations for 5 and 10.

When there are more than five dots in the Grid, ask children to tell how many blue and red dots make the total. If you ask how many are left if we take away the blue ones and how many are left if we take away the red ones, some children may come to see that if you know 5 and 2 are 7, then 7 take away 2 will always leave 5.

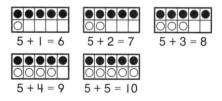

Finally, the Totally Ten Count provides a way to concretely show adding and subtracting 10. Take a full Ten Grid off the tens side and 49 becomes 39. Add a full Ten Grid, and 49 becomes 59.

HELPFUL HINT

▶ Children can create their own flash cards for 5 + 1, 5 + 2, 5 + 3, 5 + 4, and 5 + 5 by coloring dots on copies of Ten Grids (TR7) and recording facts without the sums on the back.

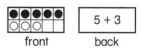

FOCUS

▶ Recognizing, analyzing, and predicting patterns
▶ Knowing the days of the week in order
▶ Counting with one-to-one correspondence
▶ Counting on and counting back
▶ Matching quantities with numerals
▶ Solving problems

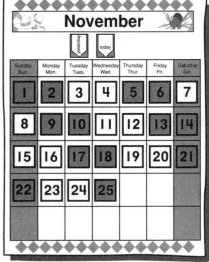

MATERIALS

Every Day Calendar, November Month Strip, November Calendar Pieces; or square shapes from Calendar Cutouts (TR21); Today and Yesterday Markers (TR21), Calendar Record (TR15)

SUGGESTED PATTERN FOR NOVEMBER

The November Calendar Pieces use orange and yellow squares to create an AABB pattern in the order orange square, orange square, yellow square, yellow square. If you choose to use the squares from the Calendar Cutouts (TR21), you can use the same or any other color pair to create the pattern. Write the dates on the pieces before posting.

FREQUENCY

Update daily. On Monday, add pieces for Saturday and Sunday. Once a week allow time for children to share their observations and to translate the month's pattern into body motions or into pattern trains with materials.

UPDATE PROCEDURE

Display the name of the month above the Calendar and help the class read it aloud. Each day as you add a Calendar Piece, help the class read the day of the week and date using the Calendar. Place the Today Marker above the day's name to highlight the day of the week and then mark the previous day of the week with the Yesterday Marker.

After a week or more, ask children to predict what color the day's piece will be and invite one or two to share their strategies for figuring this out. Continue to have children record the month's pattern on their own Calendar Record (TR15).

DISCUSSION FOR THE THIRD WEEK

Explain that a new pattern has begun to appear on the November Calendar. Refer to September's Discussion for sample questions (page 8). Ask volunteers to predict the color of a piece for a future date and justify their predictions.

Continue to encourage children to suggest ways of interpreting the month's pattern using body motions. For example, someone might suggest jumping on orange and tapping knees on yellow. Let children suggest and try out two or three different interpretations of the pattern within a session.

Provide a time at least once during the month for children to line up pattern "trains" which reflect the AABB pattern appearing on the Calendar. Some can copy and extend the November color pattern with colored paper pieces, crayons, or blocks. Others can translate the AABB pattern to colors of their choice.

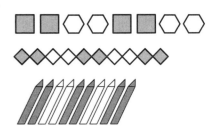

DISCUSSION FOR THE END OF THE MONTH

To wrap up the month's discussion of the Calendar pattern, ask children to tell some of the things they have noticed about the Calendar this month. Some of their responses may include:

▶ "The pattern was orange, orange, yellow, yellow."
▶ "They all go down like stairs this time."
▶ "It goes two of a kind, two of a kind, over and over."

You may want to write their observations on a large sheet of paper and attach a Calendar Record with the pattern colored in.

HELPFUL HINTS

▶ Some teachers display end-of-the-month observation records in the room or hallway. If collected throughout the year, they can be made into a Big Book of Calendar Patterns.
▶ Sometimes, when you are chanting the color pattern on the Calendar or doing body motions to the pattern, switch over to saying AABB, AABB.

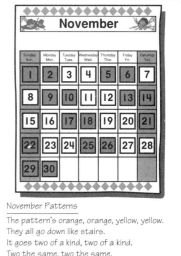

November Patterns

The pattern's orange, orange, yellow, yellow.
They all go down like stairs.
It goes two of a kind, two of a kind.
Two the same, two the same.
The oranges go 1, 2, 5, 6, 9, 10, 13,
14, 17, 18, 21, 22, 25, 26, 29, 30.
It's an A A B B, A A B B pattern.

EVERY DAY ELEMENT   BIRTHDAY DATA

FOCUS

▶ Knowing the months of the year in order
▶ Counting, comparing, and ordering small quantities
▶ Counting with one-to-one correspondence to 30
▶ Reading, comparing, and ordering numbers to 30
▶ Solving word problems and using mental math

The MATERIALS and FREQUENCY for the Birthday Data continue from October. See pages 18 and 19 for a detailed description.

UPDATE PROCEDURE

At the beginning of November, ask the class to point out the Birthday Package that matches the month written above the Calendar. Once again, have the class name all the months in order, beginning this chant with the January Package. Then go through the sequence again, stopping with a clap on the present month. Note that November is the next to last (11th) month of the year. Mention those children with birthdays this month, as indicated by the tags on the Package.

Take November's Package out of the array and feature it near the Calendar. The class can predict where the birthdays will appear on the Calendar and mark them with the tags taken from the Birthday Package. See September, page 10 for some suggested discussion questions.

DISCUSSION DURING THE MONTH

Occasionally, ask children to figure how many days until the next birthday. How much older is one November birthday child than another? Listen to those willing to share how they came to their conclusions. The lineup of Packages offers an ever-present invitation to make comparisons, count, add, and subtract. They can be used as a sponge activity when there is a minute or two at transition periods. At these times, some questions might include:

▶ Are there more birthdays this month or in your birthday month?

▶ How many birthdays come in March and April?

▶ Which month is the sixth month of the year?

▶ How many months until your birthday month arrives?

▶ How many fewer birthdays are in September than October?

▶ I see 2 months next to each other where the tags have a sum of 7. Which 2 months could these be?

▶ I see 3 months in a row which have 6 tags all together. Can you find these 3 months in a row?

EVERY DAY ELEMENT

COIN COUNTER

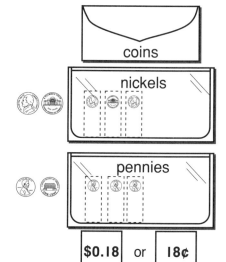

FOCUS

▶ Knowing the penny and nickel

▶ Knowing the value of each coin and coin equivalencies

▶ Counting by 10's, 5's, and 1's

▶ Determining the value of a collection of coins

▶ Using mental math, including figuring change

▶ Recording money amounts using both the dollar sign and decimal point and the cents sign

▶ Solving problems with coins

MATERIALS

Two 3" x 6" clear pockets, one labeled *nickels* and one labeled *pennies*; Penny and Nickel Demonstration Coins, or copies of Demo Coins (TR19 and 20); 6 nickel and 10 penny Coin Cards (TR3), or the same number of real nickels and pennies

OVERVIEW

As children learn the value of the coins, one of the difficulties they face is counting money by 10's, 5's, and 1's, in varying combinations. The Coin Counter activities develop this skill incrementally. In November, the penny and nickel are introduced. Adding a penny to the Coin Counter each day of the month, children represent the date in nickels and pennies, trading five pennies for a nickel whenever possible. In January, combinations of dimes, nickels, and pennies are used to create the total for the day with fewest coins. Later in the year, problem solving is the focus as children come up with a variety of coin combinations to make each date of the month. Making change for purchases made with a quarter or with 50 cents also becomes part of the routine.

FREQUENCY
Update daily and discuss once a week.

UPDATE PROCEDURE
Update the Coin Counter by placing one penny at a time into the penny pocket for each day of the month up to the present one. From this day on, add a penny a day. On Mondays add pennies for Saturday, Sunday, and Monday. When five pennies accumulate, take them out and trade them for a nickel to put into the nickel pocket. When the next penny is added, model counting the nickel as five and counting on one more (5, 6). Throughout the month, continue trading for a nickel whenever possible and counting the total each day by 5's and 1's. Record the total cents below the Coin Counter in both the dollar sign and decimal point form and the cent sign form so the children can become familiar with each.

DISCUSSION FOR THE FIRST DAY

As early in the month as possible, introduce the coins. Display the Large Demonstration Coins that show both sides of the nickel and the penny and give a real nickel and penny to each child. Ask children to look at the coins in their hands and the pictures to find some things that are alike on the nickel and penny. (Their observations will give you some openings to interject information about the two Presidents, the buildings, and the coins.)

When asked to search for ways their nickel and penny were alike, children in a first grade in Portland, Oregon, offered a variety of comments:

SAMPLE DISCUSSION

Child: They both have faces.
Child: The penny is Lincoln.
Child: The other one is Washington.
Teacher: No. George Washington, our country's very first President, is on the quarter. The face on the nickel is Thomas Jefferson, the third President. He lived at the same time as George Washington, over 200 years ago.
Child: They both have buildings.
Child: They're where the men lived.
Teacher: That is true for the nickel. Let's look at the building on the back of the nickel. The building is Jefferson's home at Monticello, Virginia. It's where he lived except for when he lived in the White House when he was President. Now, look at the building on the penny. It is the Lincoln Memorial, built 50 years after President Lincoln died, to honor him and his ideas. He was president over 125 years ago when two parts of our country were at war with each other. President Lincoln wanted the country to become reunited. There is a famous statue of Lincoln inside the memorial that many people go to see when they visit Washington, D.C. So the nickel and penny both show people and buildings. Are they alike in any other ways?
Child: They both have numbers.
Child: The numbers tell when they were made.
Child: They both say "In God We Trust."

After learning a little about the people and the buildings imprinted on the coins and exploring so many likenesses, the children shifted their focus.

SAMPLE DISCUSSION

Teacher: Now can we find some ways the nickel and penny are different?

Child: The nickel is bigger.

Child: They are different colors.

Teacher: Yes, the orange-brown penny is covered with copper metal which gives it this color. The nickel is covered with nickel metal which gives it the silver-gray color.

Child: Jefferson's house has a round top, and the building on the penny is flat on the top.

Child: "In God We Trust," is on the side of the nickel and on the top of the penny.

Child: Jefferson's hair is long and tied back. Lincoln's is short.

Teacher: Yes, it was the custom in Jefferson's time for men to wear a wig which they pulled back and tied with a ribbon.

Discuss similiarities and differences between the coins. Getting to know the nickel and penny in this way, while time consuming, should help children keep the coins straight later when they are working with dimes and quarters as well. To wrap up such a discussion, collect the nickels and pennies from the children for future use in the Coin Counter. Involve the class in updating the Coin Counter to the present day's date.

You might end by asking them to be thinking about how many nickels will collect in the nickel pocket by the end of the month. Suggest that they keep their ideas to themselves so everyone will have a chance to think about this on their own.

DISCUSSION LATER IN THE MONTH

Asking some of the following questions now and then during the month will make the Coin Counter a focus for mathematical thinking.

▶ How many coins are in our Counter?

▶ How many more days until we get the next nickel?

▶ How many days until we have 20¢?

▶ How many pennies can you get for 2 nickels?

▶ How many nickels and how many pennies were (or will be) in our Coin Counter on the 17th?

▶ If you were to take today's money from the Coin Counter to the store, would you have enough to buy something for 20¢? If I buy a pencil for 12¢, how much will I have left?

HELPFUL HINTS

▶ The use of real coins is encouraged whenever possible. Telling the class you trust them to take care of your coins so that they can be used over and over during the year may help the class to meet your expectations.

▶ First graders can't relate to the 200 years ago that Jefferson lived or the 125 years ago of Lincoln's time. However, sharing picture books about them and life in their respective eras might pique some of the children's interest.

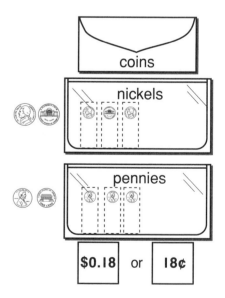

DAILY DEPOSITOR AND NUMBER STORIES

FOCUS

▶ Understanding processes of addition and subtraction

▶ Using the language of addition and subtraction and comparison

▶ Discussing combinations for sets of 0 through 10

▶ Seeing patterns in addition and subtraction

▶ Using symbolic notation to record addition and subtraction

▶ Matching quantities and numerals

▶ Understanding place value

▶ Sharing number stories to relate two small quantities to each other

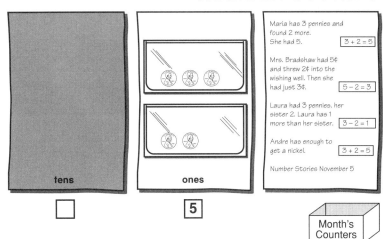

MATERIALS

$8\frac{1}{2}$" × 14" white paper for the ones place, $8\frac{1}{2}$" × 14" dark construction paper for the tens place, two 3" × 6" clear pockets attached to the ones place, three 3" × 6" clear pockets to attach as needed to the tens place, $8\frac{1}{2}$" × 14" reusable laminated record sheets (or a supply of paper record sheets placed to the right of the Depositor), 0–9 Digit Cards (TR4) for recording tens and ones below the Depositor, 30 pennies or other counters

OVERVIEW

The Daily Depositor displays a number of counters, grouped by 10's and 1's, equal to the day's date. Starting on the first of the month, a volunteer adds a counter each day to the ones side of the Depositor, which has 2 clear pockets. Counters can be placed in either pocket as they accumulate. This presents the class with a changing visual display of different combinations for 0 through 10, which supports a major goal of the Depositor.

The main purpose of this activity is to help children see and talk about addition and subtraction combinations to 10. The emphasis is on the teacher and children offering addition, subtraction, and comparison stories that go with the sets appearing in the two pockets.

When the discussions are open-ended and divergent thinking develops, the counters in the pockets may sometimes spark stories that reveal different relationships. It is important to be open to any stories that describe relationships children see. Recording one or two stories each day with both words and numbers helps children begin to connect their stories to symbolic notation.

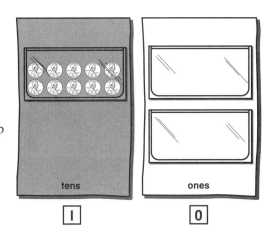

On the tenth of the month when 10 counters are collected in the 2 pockets on the ones side, they are gathered into one group of ten which is moved to a pocket on the tens side. So, on the 10th, 20th, and 30th days of the month, children are also given more exposure to place value. On these days, stories for 10 are shared orally (and not recorded) since the combinations will not remain on the ones side during the day.

FREQUENCY

Update daily with a brief discussion. On Mondays, always add two extra counters for Saturday and Sunday so the total in the Depositor is always the same as the day's date. In November, allow for extended discussion on the days when combinations for 4 and 5 appear (November 4, 5, 14, 15, 24, and 25).

UPDATE PROCEDURE

Each day of the month, a volunteer places a counter in one or the other of the two clear pockets on the ones side of the Depositor. Children share stories which are recorded and read back by the class. Whenever 10 counters accumulate, put them into a new pocket on the tens side. Each day, record the total in tens and ones, or expanded notation.

DISCUSSION THROUGHOUT THE MONTH

Each day involve the class briefly in listening to one or two stories relating the two sets of counters on the ones side, recording a story in words and with math symbols, and reading the notation back in everyday language.

Listen to two or three children share their addition and subtraction, comparison, or other kinds of stories which describe the way the counters are grouped in the two pockets. On November 17, for example, the first 10 counters will have been regrouped on the tens side, and there will be 7 counters on the ones side. If 3 pennies are in the top pocket and 4 are below, one child's story might be, "I found 3 pennies last week and 4 this week. So now I have 7." Record a paraphrased version of the story in words on a large record sheet along with a symbolic number sentence, in this case, 3 + 4 = 7.

Help the class read the number sentence back using everyday language. Linking everyday words that children readily understand to the math notation helps them see that symbolic math is nothing mysterious. Formal math terms can be used interchangeably with everyday language as the year goes on so children pick up their meanings over time.

DISCUSSION FOR DAYS WITH FOUR OR FIVE ON THE ONES SIDE

A brief discussion allowing for one or two stories should take place daily. A few times each month it will prove worthwhile to allow time for an extended discussion in which many stories are shared. The more stories, the more likely it will be to see several related facts emerge for the day's combination. For example, on the fifth, 3 + 2 = 5, 2 + 3 = 5, 5 – 2 = 3, and 3 – 2 = 1 may all appear, or 4 + 1 = 5, 1 + 4 = 5, 5 – 1 = 4, 5 – 4 = 1, and 4 – 1 = 3, depending on the placement of the counters and the stories suggested by the class.

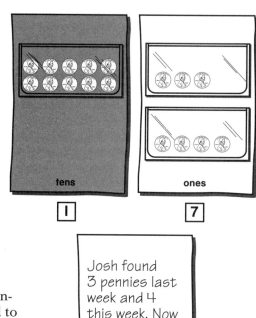

Josh found 3 pennies last week and 4 this week. Now he has 7.

3 + 4 = 7

HELPFUL HINTS

▶ Changing the objects from month to month will provide a range of storytelling situations for children to respond to. Suggestions for counters to use in place of pennies in future months include buttons, small rocks, bread tags, and canceled stamps, which children can bring from home throughout November while the pennies are in use. The following note to parents is a sample that can be adapted to fit your needs:

Dear Parents:

We will be making collections during the next few weeks which will be used for sorting, classifying, and searching for patterns in addition, subtraction, and place value. Could you help your child collect a few things from the list below?

_____ buttons   _____ canceled stamps

_____ small rocks   _____ plastic bread tags
      or shells

Please contribute only things that need not be returned. Thank you for encouraging your child to save and share some of these items with the class.

▶ On the days for extended storytelling, you may find it helpful to remove the 4 or 5 counters from the ones pockets and let children act out their stories with the counters, placing them into the pockets as they talk. The only constraint is that they use only the counters from the ones pockets. This often leads to children splitting the counters between the pockets in different ways, exposing the class to more combinations for the day's number. For example, on a day with 4 counters, 4 and 0, 3 and 1, and 2 and 2 could all appear in the pockets as the children tell a variety of number stories.

▶ Some children may need help starting stories. For these children, you might display simple pictures of coin purses or piggy banks (TR13) under the clear pockets on the ones side on the Depositor.

▶ If you record the stories on paper, they can be collected into booklets and kept in the classroom library for future browsing. Some teachers who have recorded the number sentences at the bottom of each sheet create a "flip and match book" by cutting the number sentences off the sheet, mixing up their order, and then stapling both the stories and the number sentences into a new booklet. Children can then flip through the book together and connect the stories to their matching number sentences.

Josh found 3 pennies last week and 4 this week. Now he has 7.

3 + 4 = 7

DECEMBER

WINDING DOWN THE CALENDAR YEAR

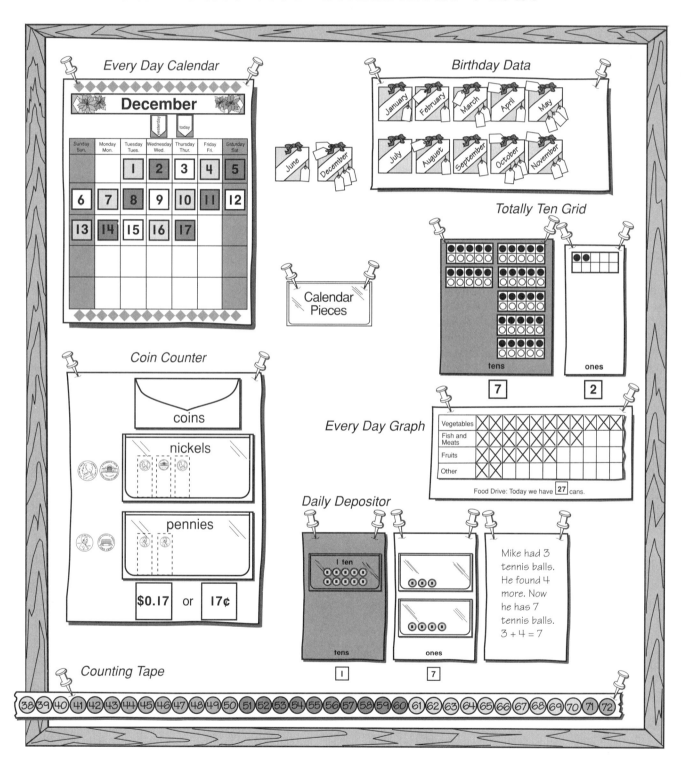

December is often hectic. To minimize teacher preparation, there are no new elements introduced this month.

You'll notice that the December holidays do not play a part in Calendar Math since views differ widely as to the role holidays should play in schools. If your school is one in which these holidays are incorporated into the classroom, you might want to adapt the Calendar and Number Stories to reflect them.

EVERY DAY ELEMENT   COUNTING TAPE

FOCUS

▶ Developing number sense
▶ Counting with one-to-one correspondence
▶ Grouping and counting by 10's and 1's
▶ Understanding place value
▶ Comparing and ordering quantities
▶ Counting on and counting back
▶ Extending number patterns and using mental math
▶ Using the language of duration
▶ Solving problems

The MATERIALS, FREQUENCY, and UPDATE PROCEDURE for the Counting Tape continue from September. See pages 2 and 3.

DISCUSSION DURING THE MONTH

As in prior months, continue to ask questions that involve children in comparing numbers, counting on, counting back, and counting by 10's and 1's. (See September, pages 3 and 4.) For example, on Day 63 some questions might include:

▶ How many more days are there until Day 70? How did some of you decide that?
▶ If today's circle shows number 63, what number is on the circle that we put up 10 days ago? Could someone share how you got your answer?
▶ Julia joined our class on Day 40. About how many days has she been part of our class? How many circles have we added to the Tape since we put up number 55? Since Day 45?

HELPFUL HINT

▶ Children enjoy using the Counting Tape to play the game *I'm Thinking of a Number*. The teacher gives clues for a number appearing on the Counting Tape, and the children use the Tape to try to figure out the number. The clues can provide different degrees of challenge. For example:

I'm thinking of a number that . . .
is 3 more than 15.
is the same as 3 groups of 10 and 4 more.
is the same as 5 and 5 and 3.
is 4 more minutes than half an hour.

60th day of school

Focus

▶ Experiencing duration
▶ Understanding analog and digital clocks
▶ Learning how many minutes in an hour
▶ Counting by 5's and 1's
▶ Reading the minute and hour hands

The MATERIALS, FREQUENCY, and UPDATE PROCEDURE for the Clock continue from September. See page 5 for a detailed description. If possible, having a digital clock or a kitchen timer will be helpful again this month.

Update Procedure for Day 60 and Beyond

On Day 60, record ":00" to show zero minutes past the new hour. From Day 61 until December vacation, begin adding minutes for a new hour, or put the Clock aside for now. It will serve a new purpose in January.

Discussion for Day 60

On Day 60, when the minute hand has finally made it all the way around the Clock, consider celebrating the concepts of one minute and one hour. This might happen by honoring each journey the minute hand makes around the classroom clock on this day by initiating one minute of silence beginning at one minute before each new hour. Children will be developing a feeling for just how long a minute is, and an hour as well. If they read the clock at 9:59, 10:59, and so on throughout the day, they will gain practice reading the hour hand when it is in its most misleading position. If time allows, some other possibilities for exploring the idea of a minute and an hour might include:

▶ Can you jog slowly in place for one whole minute?
▶ How many times can we say our ABC's in one minute?
▶ Can you tie your shoes in one minute?
▶ What lasts one hour?
▶ If you could choose something to do with your parents or family for one whole hour, what would it be?
▶ If you could choose what to do at school for an hour, what would it be?

Helpful Hints

▶ You might want to employ a kitchen timer or digital alarm clock on the 60th day to remind everyone to look at the classroom clock just prior to the arrival of each new hour.
▶ Use the classroom clock to reinforce the concept of the hour hand moving ahead just one hour each time the minute hand makes its 60-minute journey around the clock.
▶ Play the *Clock Race* game. Provide each player with a copy of the Every Day Clock (TR8) and a different color crayon. Players take turns rolling a 1–6 number cube and coloring in a matching number of minute spaces on their clock, beginning at "0." Players should switch crayons on the completion of each turn. The winner is the first player to color in all 60 minutes.

EVERY DAY ELEMENT

FOCUS

▶ Developing number sense
▶ Grouping and counting by 10's, 5's, and 1's
▶ Understanding place value
▶ Learning addition combinations for sums 5 through 10
▶ Adding or subtracting 10
▶ Using mental math

The MATERIALS, FREQUENCY, and UPDATE PROCEDURE for the Totally Ten Count continue from November. See page 25.

DISCUSSION DURING THE MONTH

As in November (page 25), continue talking about the addition combinations appearing in the Grid on the ones side and practicing adding and subtracting tens on the tens side. Try predicting how many more tens and ones are needed to fill 10 grids to reach 100.

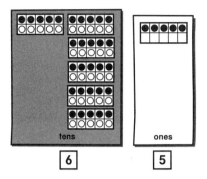

EVERY DAY ELEMENT

CALENDAR

FOCUS

▶ Recognizing, analyzing, and predicting patterns
▶ Knowing the days of the week in order
▶ Counting with one-to-one correspondence
▶ Counting on and counting back
▶ Matching quantities with numerals
▶ Solving problems

MATERIALS

Every Day Calendar, December Month Strip, December Calendar Pieces; or square shapes from Calendar Cutouts (TR21); Today and Yesterday Markers (TR21), Calendar Record (TR15)

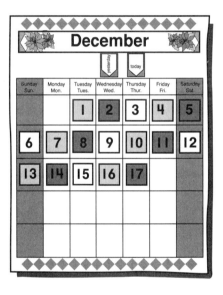

SUGGESTED PATTERN FOR DECEMBER

The December Calendar Pieces use green, blue, and red squares to create an ABC pattern in the order green square, blue square, red square. If you choose to use the squares from the Calendar Cutouts (TR21), you can use the same or any other set of three colors to create the pattern. Write the dates on the pieces before posting.

The FREQUENCY and UPDATE PROCEDURE for the Calendar continue from November. See page 26 for a detailed description. Ask the children to predict the day's color and tell the day of the week and the date. You might also add a special countdown of the remaining days in the year.

DISCUSSION FOR THE SECOND WEEK

Explain that a new pattern is beginning to appear on the December Calendar. Refer to September's Discussion for sample questions (page 8).

Interpreting the pattern with body motions may be more challenging this month, since children will need to think of three different motions to carry out the ABC pattern. (See September, page 8.) For example, someone might suggest the sequence—touch your nose, reach for the ceiling, and touch your waist.

DISCUSSION JUST PRIOR TO DECEMBER VACATION

The mid-month break for vacation offers a special opportunity for children to use their evolving understanding of patterns to help predict the rest of the month's Calendar Pieces. Pointing out the space for the last day of the month and asking, "What color will appear here?" will evoke a variety of problem-solving approaches on the children's part. Allow time for several children to show on the Calendar how they came up with their prediction. Let children predict and put up the Calendar Pieces for other December days until the entire month's pieces are up. Some children might enjoy the option of coloring and extending the pattern throughout the entire month on a December Calendar Record (TR15) to take home.

When all the pieces are up, children can share their observations as they have done in past months.

▶ "The pattern was green, blue, red, green, blue, red."
▶ "The colors repeat ABC, ABC, ABC."
▶ "There are three and three and three."
▶ "All three colors go down like stairs. The greens go 1, 7, and 13. The blues go 2, 8, 14, and 20. The reds go 3, 9, 15, 21, and 27."

HELPFUL HINT

▶ Children might enjoy making a paper chain with a link to represent each day remaining in December. Some children might want to see the month's color pattern incorporated into the chain. A link can be removed and those that are left recounted each morning. Another way to count down is to write the numbers from 1 to the total days left on an inch-squared-paper strip (TR11) and cut off or cross out one number a day until only the square labeled "1" remains on December 31. If time allows for children to make their own chain or count-down strip sometime prior to vacation, they can take it home and share the routine with their families.

December calendar grid:

Sunday Sun.	Monday Mon.	Tuesday Tues.	Wednesday Wed.	Thursday Thur.	Friday Fri.	Saturday Sat.
		1	2	3	4	5
6	7	8	9	10	11	12
13	14	15	16	17	18	19
20	21	22	23	24	25	26
27	28	29	30	31		

Number strip: 1 2 3 4 5 6 7 8 9 10 11 12 13 14 ~~15~~ ~~16~~

EVERY DAY ELEMENT   BIRTHDAY DATA

FOCUS

▶ Knowing the months of the year in order
▶ Counting, comparing, and ordering small quantities
▶ Counting with one-to-one correspondence to 31
▶ Reading, comparing, and ordering numbers to 31
▶ Solving problems and using mental math
▶ Interpreting organized data

The MATERIALS and FREQUENCY for the Birthday Data continue from September and October. See page 9 and page 18 for a detailed description.

UPDATE PROCEDURE
At the beginning of December, ask the class to point out the Birthday Package that matches the month written above the Calendar. Have the class name all the months in order, beginning this chant with the January Package. Then go through the sequence again, stopping with a clap on the present month. Note that December is the 12th and last month of the year. After reminding everyone of this year's number, let children predict the number for the new year which will appear when everyone returns from their December break.

After looking at all the months together, take December's package out of the array and feature it near the Calendar. If you have decided to recognize summer vacation birthdays on those children's half-year birthdays, you will need to bring down the June Package as well. (See September Helpful Hints, page 10.) The class can predict where the birthdays and half-year "unbirthdays" will appear on the Calendar and mark them with the tags taken from the Birthday Packages.

DISCUSSION FOR THE BEGINNING OF THE MONTH
See September, page 10, for some possible questions to accompany the identification of the month's birthdays on the Calendar.

DISCUSSION DURING THE MONTH
In addition to occasionally asking, "How many days until the next birthday?" ask, "How many days until the year ends?" to bring attention to the windng down of one calendar year and the upcoming New Year beginning January 1.

HELPFUL HINT
▶ Agree on a day just prior to vacation to recognize any children whose birthdays will occur during vacation. Any children who have a January birthday before school resumes can be recognized on the first day back from vacation, when the January Package is brought down from the array and its tags are placed on the January Calendar.

EVERY DAY ELEMENT

COIN COUNTER

FOCUS

- ▶ Knowing the penny and nickel
- ▶ Knowing the value of each coin and coin equivalencies
- ▶ Counting by 10's, 5's, and 1's
- ▶ Determining the value of a collection of coins
- ▶ Using mental math, including figuring change
- ▶ Recording money amounts using both the dollar sign and decimal point and the cent sign
- ▶ Problem solving with coins

The MATERIALS, FREQUENCY, and UPDATE PROCEDURE for the Coin Counter continue from November. See pages 28 and 29.

DISCUSSION DURING THE MONTH

Questions similar to any of the following will focus attention on the coins and encourage some mental math:

- ▶ How many days until we get the next nickel?
- ▶ How much will we have on that day?
- ▶ How many nickels and pennies will there be on the 19th?
- ▶ If we take today's money to the store, can we buy a pencil for 8¢? What will our change be?
- ▶ How much more do we need to buy a sharpener for 25¢?

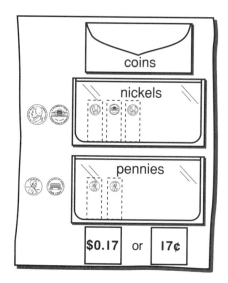

EVERY DAY ELEMENT

DAILY DEPOSITOR AND NUMBER STORIES

FOCUS

- ▶ Understanding processes of addition and subtraction
- ▶ Using the language of addition and subtraction and comparison
- ▶ Discussing part and whole relationships for the sets to 10
- ▶ Seeing patterns in addition and subtraction
- ▶ Using symbolic notation to record addition and subtraction
- ▶ Matching quantities and numerals
- ▶ Understanding place value
- ▶ Sharing number stories to relate two small quantities to each other

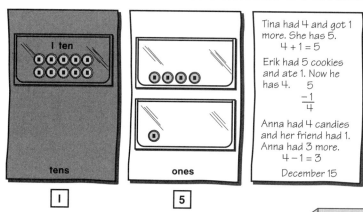

MATERIALS

The Depositor (from November), 31 buttons or other counters

FREQUENCY

Update daily. On Mondays, always add two extra counters for Saturday and Sunday so the total in the Depositor is always the same as the day's date. In December, try to allow for extended discussion when combinations for 5 and 6 appear on the ones side (December 5, 6, 15, and 16).

The UPDATE PROCEDURE for the Daily Depositor and Number Stories continues from November. See page 32.

DISCUSSION DURING THE MONTH

Refer to November's Discussion for specific details (page 32). Following the focus on 4's and 5's in November, we suggest choosing days in December when 5 or 6 counters are on the ones side for these extended discussions.

HELPFUL HINT

▶ Children can create their own number storybook by coloring in their own counters and telling their own stories to a partner or parents later at home. You may want to use the Box Backgrounds (TR14).

EVERY DAY ELEMENT   GRAPH

FOCUS

▶ Collecting and recording data on a graph over time
▶ Reading and interpreting data on a picture or bar graph
▶ Counting and comparing quantities
▶ Sorting and classifying

Vegetables	X	X	X	X						
Fish and Meats	X									
Fruits	X	X	X							
Other										

Food Drive: Today we have $\boxed{9}$ cans.

MATERIALS

Every Day Graph (TR9)

OVERVIEW

Since December has fewer school days than other months, finding time to pursue a new graph for this month is difficult. However, since many school communities are committed to canned food drives for charity at this time of year, we offer some suggestions for sorting and graphing such a collection. If children bring in cans for a food bank, you may be surprised at how much math they can do.

FREQUENCY

Update daily. Discuss as often as possible.

UPDATE PROCEDURE

Have children sort the cans several ways and decide upon the categories for the class graph. (See the discussion that follows.) Help them prepare the Graph in the following way: Children who have brought cans can color or place X's in the spaces so that all the cans collected so far are represented on the Graph. Have children who bring in cans on subsequent days mark them on the Graph when they enter the classroom.

DISCUSSION FOR THE FIRST DAY

Instead of preparing a Canned Foods Graph ahead of time, consider involving children in sorting the collection of cans several ways and then deciding which kind of sorting they would like to show on a class graph.

Following the children's suggestions, sort the cans many times. To get them started, you can ask them to look at the collection and offer one thing they notice about the cans. For example, one child says that some cans are big and others are small, leading to sorting the cans by size. Another mentions that some of them have red labels, leading to sorting by color. Someone notices that some of the cans are soups, resulting in sorting the cans by content. After sorting many ways, children can choose to graph the cans into the categories suggested by one of the sortings.

Here is an example of one such sorting experience with children:

SAMPLE DISCUSSION

Teacher: Let's look at these cans which have been brought in so far. Raise your hand if you would be willing to tell us one thing you notice about the cans.

Child: Two are soup.

Teacher: Yes, let's put all the soups over here, and leave the ones that are not soup over there. Which do we have more of, soups or not soups?

Child: Not soups.

Teacher: Let's put the cans back together. What else do you notice about the cans?

Child: Some have pictures of the foods on them.

Teacher: Let's sort by pictures and no pictures. Which group has fewer cans?

Child: No pictures.

Teacher: We'll put them back together again. What else do you notice about the cans?

Child: They are different colors.

Teacher: Yes. Could you come sort them by their colors? What should we do with this one that has both yellow and green on it?

Child: Let's not count the picture on the front, just the paper.

Teacher: All right. We'll go by the main color on the label and not count the picture. How many different color groups did we wind up with?

Child: Five.

Teacher: Are there the same number of cans in any of these groups?

Child: The reds and the greens both have four.

Teacher: Let's put them all together again. What else do you notice?

Child: The pineapple and peaches are fruits.

Teacher: Let's put the fruits together. How many vegetables do we have?

Child: We have five cans for the vegetables. What about the chicken soup? It has some vegetables.

Teacher: We may need a category for foods that have both vegetables and other ingredients.

Child: There's a can of tuna left.

Teacher: Tuna is a fish. We can have a place for high protein foods like fish, chicken, and other meats. Our bodies need a certain amount of protein each day, so food banks like to get plenty of high protein foods. So far we have a place for fruits, vegetables, fish and meats, and mixed ingredients. Which group has the most cans today?

Class: Vegetables.

Teacher: How many cans have been brought in so far?

Vegetables	X	X	X	X				
Fish and Meats	X							
Fruits	X	X	X					
Other								

Food Drive: Today we have 9 cans.

DISCUSSION LATER IN THE MONTH

Once or twice a week focus on the Graph that the class has constructed to keep track of the chosen categories of cans. Ask some questions that involve children in analyzing the data. For example:

▶ What are some of the things we know from looking at our Graph?

▶ How many cans have we collected so far? How did you figure out the total? Did someone else get the total another way?

▶ How many do you think we'll have by vacation?

▶ What do we have the most of at this time? The least of?

▶ How many more _____ do we have than _____?

▶ I see two kinds of cans on the Graph that add up to _____ cans. Which two kinds are they?

▶ If we were to group the cans into stacks of 10, how many stacks of 10 would we be able to make? How many cans would be left? (Volunteers will enjoy finding cans of suitable sizes to create triangular arrangements of 10 cans with 4 in the bottom layer and 3, 2, and then 1 stacked on top.)

HELPFUL HINTS

▶ One favorite canned food activity is sorting—by sizes, by colors, even by the beginning sounds of the contents. For the latter activity, it may be helpful to put out some phonics picture cards. Then children can try to match the cans with the beginning sounds represented by the object in each picture. Soup cans may wind up next to the "S" picture of the sun, tuna by the "T" turtle picture, and so on.

▶ If you have access to a balance scale, this might be a great time to put it out with a few of the cans. Make it a rule that only one can can be placed on a side. Ask children to choose two cans, lift them, and guess which is heavier. Then have them place the cans on the scale to check their guess.

▶ Cans labeled with pretend prices (less than 50¢) arranged on a shelf with some coin purses or envelopes of play money coins will create an instant play store. Children enjoy playing out the roles of consumers and clerks.

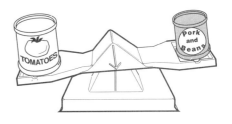

JANUARY

STARTING AGAIN

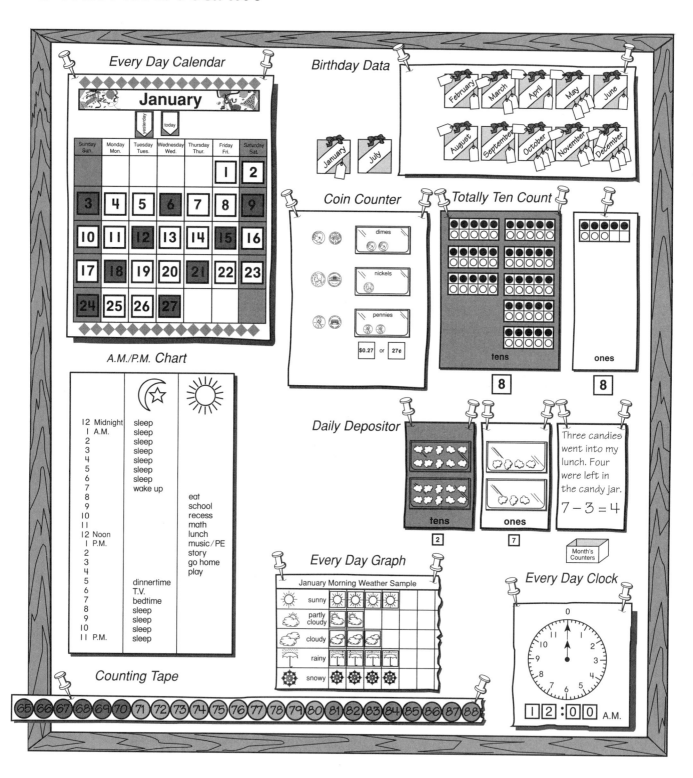

In January, the Clock changes from showing the number of school days in minutes to reflecting the month's date in hours. The Coin Counter now has a dime pocket along with the nickel and penny pockets. The Daily Depositor with accompanying Number Stories provides more experience in adding, subtracting, and comparing small quantities. The Counting Tape and the Totally Ten Count focus attention on the question, "How many more until we have 100?" as Day 100 draws near.

EVERY DAY ELEMENT   COUNTING TAPE

FOCUS

▶ Developing number sense
▶ Counting with one-to-one correspondence
▶ Grouping and counting by 10's and 1's
▶ Understanding place value
▶ Comparing and ordering quantities
▶ Counting on and counting back
▶ Extending number patterns and using mental math
▶ Using the language of duration
▶ Solving problems

The MATERIALS, FREQUENCY, and UPDATE PROCEDURE for the Counting Tape continue from September. See pages 2 and 3 for a detailed description.

DISCUSSION DURING THE MONTH

As in prior months, continue asking questions which foster counting on, counting back, adding, comparing, grouping, and counting by 10's and 1's. (See September, pages 3 and 4.) With Day 100 approaching, the class can also consider the question of how many more school days until this special day arrives.

Encourage them to use the color pattern on the Tape to organize their counting of the 1's and 10's still to come. This strategy of "counting up" to the nearest 10 and then counting on by 10's will be useful in figuring correct change and in doing mental addition and subtraction.

HELPFUL HINT

▶ If you'd like each child to bring in a collection of 100 things to help celebrate the one hundredth day of school, it is a good idea to brainstorm ideas for possible collections a few weeks ahead. Parents are usually very willing to support such a project if they know about it ahead of time. Let children know you wouldn't want them to risk having anything of personal value lost, stolen, or broken, so they shouldn't bring in toys, money, or collections they would be upset over losing. Ask children to group or organize their objects into 10's so that everyone will be able to see the 10 tens in their hundred.

FOCUS

▶ Experiencing duration
▶ Understanding analog and digital clocks
▶ Learning how many minutes in an hour
▶ Counting by 5's and 1's
▶ Reading the minute and hour hands

MATERIALS

Every Day Clock with both the minute and hour hands attached, 9" × 12" clear pocket, A.M./P.M. Chart (TR10)

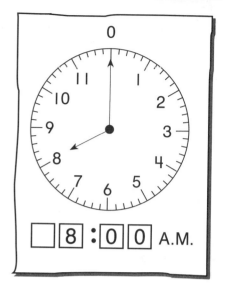

OVERVIEW

For the first 60 days of school, the Clock had only a minute hand which moved forward one minute per day. The children practiced counting by 5's and 1's and reading the minutes past any hour. Now in January, the focus switches to the shorter hour hand which is added to the Every Day Clock. The Clock is used to show each of the 24 hours in a day as the clock hands move ahead one hour on each of the first 24 days in January.

FREQUENCY

Update daily. On Monday, catch up for Saturday and Sunday. Discuss once or twice a week.

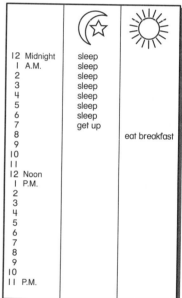

UPDATE PROCEDURE

As early in January as possible, update the Clock to the present day's date. Each day from then on, advance the Clock ahead one hour, reading the times at each 5-minute interval. This will help children to see how the hour and minute hands move simultaneously. Record an activity that would take place at that hour of the day on the A.M./P.M. Chart. On Mondays, add hours for Saturday and Sunday. On the 13th, advance to 1:00 P.M., on the 14th, to 2:00 P.M., and so on, until returning to 12:00 midnight on January 24. Put the Clock aside for the remainder of the month.

DISCUSSION FOR THE FIRST DAY

Begin with the hands of the Clock pointing straight up, showing 12:00 midnight. Explain to the children that each new day begins at 12:00 midnight in the middle of the night. On the A.M./P.M. Chart, record what the children are doing at this time of day—sleeping, most likely. Ask them to count the minutes by 5's as you advance the minute hand through 60 minutes and move the hour hand slowly ahead to 1:00 A.M. (12:05, 12:10, 12:15 . . .). Ask how many minutes passed while the short hour hand moved ahead one hour to 1:00 A.M. By the time children have watched this 24 times, they will begin to see the relationship between the long minute hand going around once and the short hour hand advancing just one hour. Again record what the class is doing at 1:00 A.M. on the Chart. Continue to advance the hands of the Clock one hour for each day of January, recording an activity for each of these hours on the Chart.

DISCUSSION LATER IN THE MONTH

On the 11th, stop when the classroom clock shows 11:00 A.M. and ask the class to determine what time it was one hour ago and what was happening then. Then do the same for 2 hours ago, 3 hours ago, and so on.

Also, ask what time it will be in 1 more hour, 2 more hours, 3 more hours, and so on. On the 12th, stop at 12:00 noon and point out the change from A.M. to P.M. Continue on the 13th to stop at 1:00 P.M. and on the 14th to stop at 2:00 P.M. and ask questions requiring children to go back or go ahead a few hours.

HELPFUL HINT

▶ Some classes have enjoyed adding a tally of their favorite hours of the day to the A.M./P.M. Chart. On January 25, children study the Chart and review the various activities listed for the different hours of the day. They write down their favorite hour on a slip of paper (without consulting their classmates). The slips are collected and read out loud as the teacher places a tally mark to the left of each time as it is announced. Are more of the favorite hours within the school day or outside school hours? Are more during daylight or darkness? Are more of the favorite times A.M. or P.M. times?

EVERY DAY ELEMENT

TOTALLY TEN COUNT

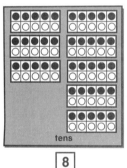 

8   7

FOCUS

▶ Developing number sense
▶ Grouping and counting by 10's, 5's, and 1's
▶ Understanding place value
▶ Learning addition combinations for sums 5 through 10
▶ Adding or subtracting 10
▶ Using mental math

The MATERIALS, FREQUENCY, and UPDATE PROCEDURE for the Totally Ten Count continue from November. See page 25 for a detailed description.

DISCUSSION DURING THE MONTH

As in November (page 25), continue to talk about the addition combinations for 5 and 10 that appear in the Grid on the ones side, and practice adding and subtracting 10's on the tens side. With Day 100 approaching, ask the class to predict how many more 10's and 1's are needed to fill 10 of the Grids to make 100.

HELPFUL HINT

▶ Play *Fill Up Tens to 50*. Players will need 100 pennies and a 1–6 dot cube. Each player uses 5 ten grids from the Totally Ten Grids (TR7). Players take turns tossing the cube and placing that number of pennies on a grid. The grids should be filled left to right across the top and then across the bottom. Players must tell how many counters they have in all before each toss. The first player to fill five grids wins.

FOCUS

▶ Recognizing, analyzing, and predicting patterns
▶ Knowing the days of the week in order
▶ Counting with one-to-one correspondence
▶ Counting on and counting back
▶ Matching quantities with numerals
▶ Solving problems

MATERIALS

Every Day Calendar, January Month Strip, January Calendar Pieces; or square shapes from Calendar Cutouts (TR21); Today and Yesterday Markers (TR21), Calendar Record (TR15)

SUGGESTED PATTERN FOR JANUARY

The January Calendar Pieces use white and green squares to create an AAB pattern in the order white square, white square, green square. If you choose to use the squares from the Calendar Cutouts (TR21), you can use the same or any other pair of colors to create the pattern. Write the dates on the pieces before posting.

The FREQUENCY and UPDATE PROCEDURE for the Calendar continue from November. See page 26 for a detailed description.

DISCUSSION FOR THE THIRD WEEK

Explain that a new pattern is beginning to appear on the January Calendar. Refer to September's discussion for sample questions (page 8).

The children will need to think of only two different motions to carry out the AAB pattern with body motions this month (see September, page 8). Let children suggest and try several interpretations for the basic AAB pattern within one discussion period. At other times, let children use various art materials to create an AAB pattern of their own.

DISCUSSION FOR THE END OF THE MONTH

On one of the last days of January, ask children to look for some patterns to share with the class. You might want to record their observations on a large sheet of paper.

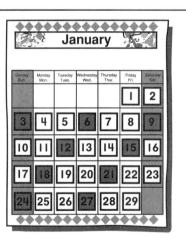

The greens go 3, 6, 9, 12, 15, 18, 21, 24, 27.

It goes white, white, green over and over.

It's an A A B pattern.

One staircase goes down 6, 12, 18, 24. The other green steps go 9, 15, 21, 27.

I see 1,2; 4,5; 7,8; 10,11; 13,14 ...

I see two green diagonals and a green in one corner all alone.

FOCUS

▶ Knowing the months of the year in order
▶ Counting, comparing, and ordering small quantities
▶ Counting with one-to-one correspondence to 31
▶ Reading, comparing, and ordering numbers to 31
▶ Solving problems and using mental math
▶ Interpreting organized data

The MATERIALS and FREQUENCY for the Birthday Data continue from September and October. See page 9 and page 18 for a detailed description.

UPDATE PROCEDURE

At the beginning of January, ask the class to point out the Birthday Package that matches the month written above the Calendar. Have the class name all the months in order, beginning with the January Package. Begin again with January, stopping with a clap on this month. Note that January is the first month of the new year. After reminding everyone of this year's new number, let children practice reading and writing it.

After looking at all the months together, take January's Package out of the array and feature it near the Calendar. If you have decided to recognize summer vacation birthdays on the children's half-year birthdays, you will need to bring down the July Package as well. (See September Helpful Hints, page 10.) The class can predict where the birthdays and half-year "unbirthdays" will appear on the Calendar and mark them with the tags.

DISCUSSION FOR THE BEGINNING OF THE MONTH

See September, page 10, for some possible questions to accompany the identification of the month's birthdays on the Calendar. A special tag can be placed on January 15 to note the birthday of Dr. Martin Luther King, Jr.

DISCUSSING DURING THE MONTH

Ask children to try to find the Birthday packages you are thinking of when you provide hints similar to the following:

▶ "I am thinking of 2 months that have 6 birthdays in all."
▶ "I am thinking of 2 months. One of them has 3 more birthdays than the other, and together they have 5 birthdays in all."
▶ "I am thinking of 2 months. One has 4 more birthdays than the other."

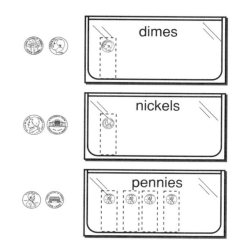

FOCUS

▶ Knowing the penny, nickel, and dime
▶ Knowing the value of each coin and coin equivalencies
▶ Counting by 10's, 5's, and 1's
▶ Determining the value of a collection of coins
▶ Using mental math, including figuring change
▶ Recording money amounts using both the dollar sign and decimal point and the cent sign
▶ Problem solving with coins

MATERIALS

The MATERIALS for the Coin Counter continue from November. See page 28 for a detailed description. In addition, add a clear pocket labeled *dimes* to the Coin Counter display on the bulletin board. Also, the Dime Demonstration Card should be added to the display and copies of dime Coin Cards (TR3) or real dimes will be needed.

OVERVIEW

In January, the Coin Counter gives children experience in trading 5 pennies for a nickel and 2 nickels for a dime as they add 1¢ each day of the month. As they count out the total value of the coins each day, they get practice in counting by 10's, 5's, and 1's—a skill difficult for some first graders.

FREQUENCY

Update daily and discuss once a week.

UPDATE PROCEDURE

Catch up to the day's date by placing one penny at a time into the penny pocket for each day up to the present one. From this day on, add a penny a day. On Mondays, add pennies for Saturday, Sunday, and Monday. Whenever 5 pennies accumulate, take them out and trade them for a nickel to put into the nickel pocket. When the next penny is added, model counting the nickel as 5 and count on one more (5, 6). When the second nickel is earned on the tenth, trade both nickels in for a dime and place it in the dime pocket. Throughout the month, continue trading for nickels and dimes whenever possible. Count each day's total by 10's and 1's or by 10's, 5's, and 1's. For example, on January 19, children would count, "10, 15, 16, 17, 18, 19." Record the total cents below the Coin Counter in both the dollar sign and decimal point and the cent sign forms.

DISCUSSION FOR THE BEGINNING OF THE MONTH

As early in the month as possible, introduce the dime. Identify its value as 10¢. Add the large Dime Demo Coins to the display of the nickel and penny Demo Coins next to the Coin Counter. Pass out a dime to each child. Ask children to look at the dime to find some things that make it different from the nickel and the penny. Their observations may give you the opportunity to tell them a little bit about Franklin Roosevelt and the torch of liberty between sprigs of laurel and oak.

Following the discussion, collect the dimes and use the Update Procedure described to catch the Coin Counter up to the day's date.

DISCUSSION LATER IN THE MONTH

Asking some of the following questions during the month may help develop some children's mental math:

▶ How many coins are in the Counter?

▶ How many more days until we get the next nickel?

▶ How many more days until we get the next dime?

▶ How many days until we have 20¢? 30¢?

▶ How many pennies can you get for 2 nickels? 3 nickels?

▶ What coins do you think will be in the Counter on the 8th? On the 11th? On the 15th? On the 17th? On the 20th?

▶ If you were to take today's money from the Coin Counter to the store, would you have enough to buy something that costs 10¢? 15¢? 25¢? If you were to buy candy for 6¢, how much would you have left? What if you bought a small eraser for 16¢ instead? Sometimes invite children to enter into the discussion with store problems of their own.

HELPFUL HINTS

▶ A collection of objects labeled with prices from 5¢ to 40¢ can make the store problems more real to children.

▶ This is an excellent opportunity to let children experiment with calculators. Discuss how to add on a calculator, and allow them to confirm the cost of their purchases.

▶ When Barbara Garcia jingles her coin purse that holds nickels and pennies, some first graders in Portland, Oregon, are eager to suggest possible solutions to the open-ended problems she poses. "I have 3 coins in my purse. How many cents could they be worth?" Or she poses the opposite situation, "I have 13¢. What coins could be in this purse?" Noting the children's suggestions by drawing coins in rows on a large piece of paper may help them to see the usefulness of making a list to keep track of all the possibilities when pursuing open-ended problems. The arrangements make it easier to see that one child's suggestion—1 nickel and 8 pennies—has the same value as another's suggestion—5 pennies, 1 nickel, and 3 more pennies.

EVERY DAY ELEMENT

DAILY DEPOSITOR AND NUMBER STORIES

FOCUS

▶ Understanding processes of addition and subtraction

▶ Using the language of addition and subtraction and comparison

▶ Discussing part and whole relationships for the sets to 10

▶ Seeing patterns in addition and subtraction

▶ Using symbolic notation to record addition and subtraction

▶ Matching quantities and numerals

▶ Understanding place value

▶ Sharing number stories to relate two small quantities to each other

MATERIALS

The Depositor (from November), 31 rocks, shells, or other counters

FREQUENCY

Update daily. On Mondays, add two extra counters for Saturday and Sunday so the total in the Depositor is always the same as the day's date. In January, allow for extended discussion when combinations for 6 and 7 appear on the ones side (on January 6, 7, 16, 17, 26, and 27).

The UPDATE PROCEDURE for the Daily Depositor and Number Stories continues from November. See page 32 for a detailed description.

DISCUSSION THROUGHOUT THE MONTH

Refer to November's Discussion for specific details (page 32).

HELPFUL HINTS

▶ Again, story records can be collected into booklets and kept in the classroom library for future browsing.

▶ The rocks or shells provide great materials for sorting. To introduce the collection ask, "Can someone tell us one thing you notice about the rocks?" When a child offers, "Some are shiny," you might follow with, "Yes, some are shiny. Are they all shiny?" Then sort them into the "shiny" and "not shiny" piles. To keep suggestions coming, push the rocks back together after each sorting and ask, "Can anyone tell us something else you notice about the rocks?" Then sort accordingly. Continue re-sorting the same material as long as interest and time allow. Children will discover many ways the objects are alike and different and increase their descriptive vocabulary by listening to each other. When the objects have been sorted in one way, some teachers ask the class, "Which group has more?" or, "Which group has less?" to encourage comparing.

▶ For an in-depth discussion of ways to use collections and the environment to foster young children's sorting skills and language, see Chapter 3 of *Mathematics Their Way* by Mary Baratta-Lorton, Addison-Wesley, 1976.

EVERY DAY ELEMENT

GRAPH

FOCUS

▶ Collecting and recording data on a graph over time
▶ Reading and interpreting data on a picture or bar graph
▶ Counting and comparing small quantities

The MATERIALS, FREQUENCY, and UPDATE PROCEDURE for the Graph continue from October. See page 20.

OVERVIEW

The Every Day Graph provides a record of a weather sample in October, January, and April. Graphing the weather again this month allows the class the opportunity to compare the kinds of weather that occurred in your area in the fall with the weather that occurs in the winter.

January Morning Weather Sample

DISCUSSION FOR THE FIRST DAY

Instead of preparing the weather graph ahead of time, consider involving children in problem-solving experiences while setting it up. Tell the children you want to create a graph that has the same headings in the same order as the October Weather Graph so it will be easy to compare the information on the two graphs.

With the October Graph in view, let them tell you how to label the new January Graph. Ask if they think the same length will work out or if they think it will need to be longer or shorter and why. Place the first day's Weather Marker on the Graph.

Looking at the October Graph, ask the class to indicate by a show of hands who thinks there will be more sunny days in January than in October, fewer sunny days, or the same number. How about rainy days? More, fewer, or the same? How about snowy days? It will be interesting to see how the two weather samples compare by month's end.

DISCUSSION DURING THE MONTH

Refer to October's Discussion for sample questions (page 21).

HELPFUL HINTS

▶ After preparing a supply of Weather Markers (TR12) for the month, you may find it handy to store them in library pockets next to the Graph.

▶ If children help color the symbols, have them use the same colors that were agreed upon in October to make it easier to compare the fall and winter graphs at the end of January. Have them mark the January Graph in the same way that the October Graph was marked.

▶ If you live in an area where the winter weather is not very different from the fall weather, it might be fun to use the daily newspaper to graph the winter weather of a city in another part of the country in addition to your own winter weather. Perhaps a city could be chosen where friends or relatives of class members live who could correspond with the class or help set up correspondence with another first grade in that area. It would be fun to hear about children's winter activities in a place with a climate much different from one's own.

FEBRUARY

A MONTH FULL OF FAVORITES

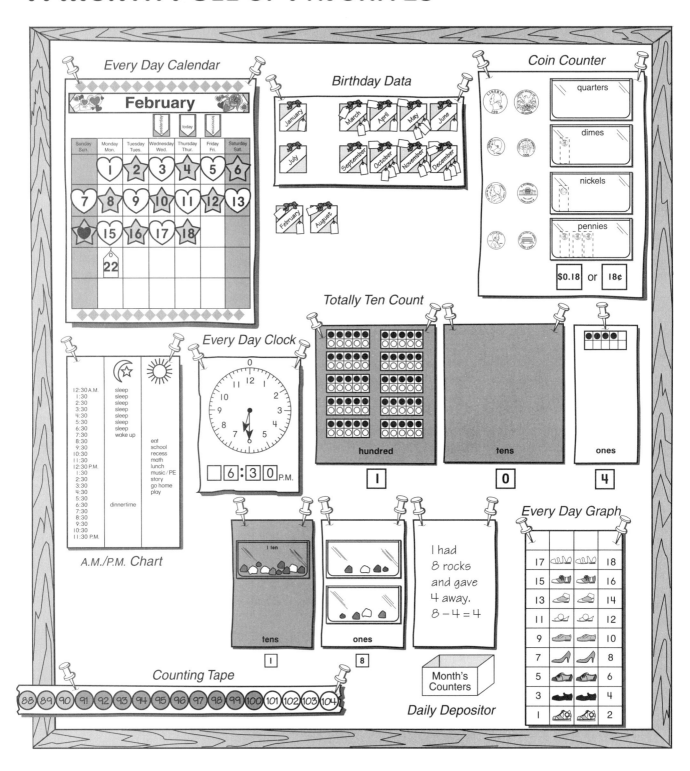

Every Day Calendar

February

Sunday Sun.	Monday Mon.	Tuesday Tues.	Wednesday Wed.	Thursday Thur.	Friday Fri.	Saturday Sat.
	1	2	3	4	5	6
7	8	9	10	11	12	13
	15	16	17	18		
22						

yesterday • today • tomorrow

Birthday Data

January • March • April • May • June

July • September • October • November • December

February • August

Coin Counter

quarters

dimes

nickels

pennies

$0.18 or 18¢

Every Day Clock

6:30 P.M.

Totally Ten Count

hundred — 1

tens — 0

ones — 4

A.M./P.M. Chart

12:30 A.M.	sleep
1:30	sleep
2:30	sleep
3:30	sleep
4:30	sleep
5:30	sleep
6:30	sleep
7:30	wake up
8:30	eat
9:30	school
10:30	recess
11:30	math
12:30 P.M.	lunch
1:30	music / PE
2:30	story
3:30	go home
4:30	play
5:30	
6:30	dinnertime
7:30	
8:30	
9:30	
10:30	
11:30 P.M.	

Daily Depositor

1 ten

tens — 1

ones — 8

I had 8 rocks and gave 4 away.
8 − 4 = 4

Month's Counters

Every Day Graph

17		18
15		16
13		14
11		12
9		10
7		8
5		6
3		4
1		2

Counting Tape

88 89 90 91 92 93 94 95 96 97 98 99 100 101 102 103 104

February brings excitement as the 100th day of school arrives. At the end of this introduction, there are some suggestions for enrichment activities to help celebrate Day 100.

This month the Counting Tape and Totally Ten Count show Day 100 drawing near. These two elements focus on this special day when the hundreds place makes its debut. The hands of the Clock will move ahead one hour each day, from 30 minutes after one hour to 30 minutes after the next. This provides practice reading the hour and minute hands.

The Calendar presents an odd and even color pattern. Birthday Data incorporates Lincoln's and Washington's birthdays and Presidents' Day. It is fitting that we add to the Coin Counter this month a pocket for quarters with George Washington imprinted on them. The Daily Depositor and Number Stories continue. Extended discussions are suggested on days when combinations for 7 or 8 appear in the ones place. The Graph in February gives attention to odd and even numbers and counting by 2's; a picture of a shoe is added each day of the month, forming even pairs every other day. Soon, children will begin to see a connection between the odd and even pattern emerging on the Graph and the color pattern on the Calendar.

LEAP YEAR

If it is a leap year or if you have a child with a February 29th birthday, you might want to mention to children that February is unique, since it gets an extra day every 4 years. A leap year happens every 4 years because each calendar year is actually all the days from January 1 to the last day in December and about 6 extra hours. When 4 years have passed, these 6 extra hours each year add up to 24 hours, thereby creating an extra day. (This day, February 29, is added every year that is divisible by 4 except centenary years not exactly divisible by 400.)

DISCUSSION FOR CELEBRATING THE ONE HUNDREDTH DAY OF SCHOOL

One hundred is a special number in our numeration system. It provides a cornerstone for understanding the base ten pattern and higher numbers. For this reason, plan to set aside some time to do a few special activities on the 100th day of school. You might choose from the following suggestions or create several of your own.

Children's Collections of 100 Objects: On Day 100, the collections can be displayed, and children can consider questions similar to those that follow:

Place Value Counting:
▶ How many collections of 100 have been brought in?
▶ How many things do you think there are in all the displays together? (List the estimates.)
▶ How could we find out? Count every one, count by 10's, or count by 100's? (When the class reaches ten 100's, explain that ten 100's make 1000.)

Estimating weight, area, and length:

▶ Which collections do you think weigh the most? Why do you think so? How could we find out?

▶ Which collections would cover the most area on a paper if the items were laid out just touching each other? Why do you think so? How could we find out?

▶ Which collections do you think would form the longest lines if the items were laid out end to end? Why do you think so? How could we find out?

Perhaps the children's predictions and ideas for verifying them could be pursued during the first few days that follow Day 100, if children keep their collections at school for a few days.

How Far Will 100 Steps Take Us? Sometime during the day on the way to the lunchroom, library, or gym, have the class guess how far 100 giant steps will take them. Then let a few at a time go ahead counting their steps as they go. Were their guesses too far, just about right, or too near?

Which Bag Has 100? Put some peanuts (in the shell) or individually wrapped candies in each of three resealable plastic bags. Make sure that one bag holds exactly 100. Invite children to guess: Which bag holds 100, Bag A, B, or C? It might be fun to tally or graph the guesses. Then assign two or three volunteers to each collection. Have them quickly group the contents of their bag into 10's so the whole class can see and count out the totals. Are the results surprising to some children? Did more children choose the bag of 100 when making their guesses or did more people choose one of the other bags? Divide the collections among class members and enjoy!

100 ROCKS

One Hundred? Prove It! Pair up children and pass out containers of different objects such as crayons, paper clips, craft sticks, toothpicks, math counters, small cubes, pegboard pegs, tiles, buttons, bread tags, small rocks, and paper squares. Give the partners a large piece of paper and ask them to decide together on a way to count out and show 100 so that others will be able to easily check their work. (Some may ask for rubber bands to bundle crayons or sticks.)

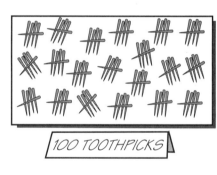

100 TOOTHPICKS

When the displays are complete, let children view one another's work and talk about some of the different ways the objects have been organized.

Creating Hundredth Day Designs: Let children use a variety of crayons to shade up to 100 squares on Blank Hundred Charts (TR23). Some will choose to create abstract designs or patterns. Others will make representational pictures. After they have been displayed awhile, gather them into a book. Children's responses to "What do you see in this design?" can be recorded on the page opposite each design. Asking, "How many squares in this design were colored red?" will encourage instant recognition of small quantities, counting on, and adding.

"I see a city. Cars and trucks are on the streets."

Josh

What Can We Do 100 Times? Some teachers break up the day with short periods of exercise. Children enjoy seeing if they can do 10 sets of 10 jumping jacks, jog or march in place 100 steps, or lean to the left and then to the right 100 times.

FOCUS

▶ Developing number sense
▶ Counting with one-to-one correspondence
▶ Grouping and counting by 10's and 1's
▶ Understanding place value
▶ Comparing and ordering quantities
▶ Counting on and counting back
▶ Extending number patterns and using mental math
▶ Solving problems

The MATERIALS, FREQUENCY, and UPDATE PROCEDURE for the Counting Tape continue from September. See pages 2 and 3 for a detailed description. Repeat the same sequence of colors used for the decades to 100 when putting up shapes for days beyond 100. Optional Materials this month include the Hundred Chart (TR16).

DISCUSSION FOR THE BEGINNING OF THE MONTH

Continue to consider the question, "How many more school days until Day 100?"

SAMPLE DISCUSSION ON DAY 100

Teacher: How many days have we been in school as of today? What comes after Day 99?
Class: One hundred.
Teacher: Yes, it is our 100th day of school, Day 100. Let's see how many complete groups of ten we have.
Teacher and Class: 1 ten to 10, 2 tens to 20, 3 tens to 30, 4 tens to 40, 5 tens to 50, 6 tens to 60, 7 tens to 70, 8 tens to 80, 9 tens to 90, and 10 tens to 100.
Teacher: Yes. Ten tens in 10 different colors. Remember how we wrote 80 with an 8 and a 0, meaning 8 tens and 0 ones, and how we wrote 90 with a 9 and a 0, meaning 9 tens and 0 ones? Watch as the pattern continues. Today I'm writing a 10 and a 0 to mean 10 tens and 0 ones. This number we read as 100 also means 10 tens. How do we usually read this number?
Class: One hundred.
Teacher: And how many groups of tens do we have?
Child: 10 tens.
Teacher: Yes. What do you think the next number will be?
Child: Two hundred.
Child: A million.
Child: One hundred and one.
Teacher: Keep thinking about it. We'll find out tomorrow (or the next school day).

DISCUSSION FOR DAY 101 AND THEREAFTER

On Day 101, when the day's shape is displayed, continue the discussion from Day 100. Focus on the number of completed 10's making up 100, and the one additional day. Some will be surprised to find out that 101 follows 100. Discuss the numbers that appear on following days in the same way.

HELPFUL HINTS

▶ If the class has been coloring the decades on the Hundred Chart (TR16) to match the colors on the Counting Tape since Day 50 (see page 24), Day 100 will be the day to complete the final row.

▶ If you have been attaching the optional yellow dot stickers to the zeros in 10, 20 . . . 90 and decorating them with the face of Zero the Hero, you'll want to make a special event of his appearing twice on Day 100. In Veronica Paracchini's primary classroom in Portland, Oregon, where Zero the Hero had been making his appearance every 10th day all year, the class celebrated Zero the Hero Day on Day 100. Children then decided that it should really be Zero the Hero Week since he kept reappearing day after day for 10 more days. Nothing like this had happened before!

▶ Some teachers arrange to have Zero the Hero visit on Day 100. Wearing a bright yellow cape, decorated with the word *Zero* and numbers with zeros in them, Zero the Hero asks about the day's special activities and leaves behind zero-shaped cereal treats for everyone.

▶ For suggestions of activities celebrating Day 100, see pages 55 and 56.

EVERY DAY ELEMENT

CLOCK

FOCUS

▶ Experiencing duration
▶ Understanding analog and digital clocks
▶ Learning how many minutes in an hour
▶ Counting by 5's and 1's
▶ Reading the minute and hour hands

The MATERIALS and FREQUENCY for the Clock continue from January. See page 46 for a detailed description.

OVERVIEW

In February, the Clock will still move ahead one hour a day, but now the focus will be on reading the Clock at the half hour. On February 1, the Clock will show 1:30 A.M.; on February 2, 2:30 A.M.; on February 3, 3:30 A.M.; and so on.

UPDATE PROCEDURE

As early in February as possible, update the Clock to the current date. (See Discussion for the First Day, page 59.) Each day from then on, slowly advance the hands of the Clock ahead one hour. Have the class read the time at each five-minute interval as the minute hand passes through 60 minutes. Each day, record the time shown on the Clock and an activity that would take place at this hour on the A.M./P.M. Chart. On Mondays, add hours for Saturday and Sunday. On the 13th, advance to 1:30 P.M., on the 14th to 2:30 P.M., and so on, until returning to 12:30 A.M. on February 24, when this activity ends for the month.

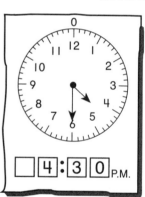

DISCUSSION FOR THE FIRST DAY

Begin with the hands of the Clock pointing to 12:30 A.M. Ask children to read the short hand and then the long minute hand. Note that the hour hand is halfway between 12:00 and 1:00. Remind children that each new day begins at 12:00 A.M. when they are asleep. On the A.M./P.M. Chart, write down what the children are doing at 12:30 A.M. Ask them to count the minutes by 5's as you advance the minute hand through 60 minutes and move the hour hand slowly ahead to show 1:30 A.M. ("12:35, 12:40, 12:45, 12:50, . . . "). Ask how many minutes passed while the hands moved ahead one hour to 1:30 A.M. Record what class members are doing at 1:30 A.M. Continue to advance the hands of the Clock one hour for each day of February up to the present day of the month, recording a typical activity for each of these items on the Chart.

DISCUSSION FOR FEBRUARY 9, 10, 11, AND 12

On the 9th, 10th, and 11th, when the Clock shows 9:30, 10:30, and 11:30 A.M., stop at these actual times during the day and read the classroom clock. To develop understanding of duration, ask the class to determine what time it was one hour ago and what was happening then. Also, ask what time it will be in one more hour. On the 12th, point out the change from A.M. to P.M. as you pass 12:00 noon.

EVERY DAY ELEMENT

TOTALLY TEN COUNT

FOCUS

- ▶ Developing number sense
- ▶ Grouping and counting by 10's, 5's, and 1's
- ▶ Understanding place value
- ▶ Learning addition combinations for sums 5 through 10
- ▶ Adding or subtracting 10
- ▶ Using mental math

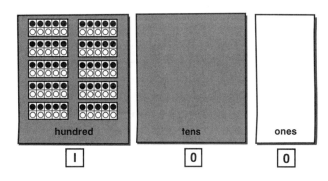

The MATERIALS, FREQUENCY, and UPDATE PROCEDURE for the Totally Ten Count continue from November. See page 25 for a detailed description. On Day 100, you will need a new piece of construction paper in a different color to provide a new tens place.

DISCUSSION FOR THE BEGINNING OF THE MONTH

As in November (see page 25), continue talking about the addition combinations for 5 and 10, which appear in the Grid in the ones place. With Day 100 approaching, ask the class to predict how many more dots are needed to fill grids to make 100.

DISCUSSION ON DAY 100

Teacher: Let's count the dots by 10's.

Class: 10, 20, 30 . . . 100.

Teacher: Yes. Today we finally have 100. How many full 10 grids did it take to make 100? Let's count them.

Class: 1 ten, 2 tens, 3 tens . . . 10 tens.

Teacher: So 10 tens make 100. Do you remember that a grid filled with 10 dots is special enough to be moved over to its own tens place? Well, when 10 Totally Ten Grids become filled, the new 100 is special enough to get its own place too. We'll move our paper with 100 on it to the hundreds place. We'll put up a fresh tens-place paper and keep the white paper for the ones place to the right of it. Now how many places do we have?

Class: 3.

Teacher: Yes. We call them the ones, tens, and hundreds places. Now what should I write under each place? How many complete hundreds do we have?

Class: 1.

Teacher: Yes, so I'll write a 1 under the hundreds place to show we have just one hundred. How many filled tens do you see in our new tens place?

Class: None.

Teacher: Yes, so I'll write a 0 under the tens place to show we have no extra tens. How many dots are on the empty grid attached to the ones place?

Class: None.

Teacher: So, I'll record a 0 under the ones place to show we have no extra ones. We can read 100 as, "One hundred, zero tens, and zero ones, or one hundred." Now let's all read it.

Class: One hundred, zero tens, and zero ones, or one hundred.

Teacher: I wonder how many dots we'll have all together on our next day of school when we add another dot? Think about it for a moment. Whisper your guess to someone sitting near you and let them whisper their guess to you. Do you agree or disagree? We'll find out tomorrow (or the next school day).

DISCUSSION FOR DAY 101 AND THEREAFTER

Continue with discussions similar to the one for Day 100, focusing on recording and reading back the number of hundreds, tens, and ones that appear in each of three places.

HELPFUL HINTS

▶ To save space, some teachers cut apart the arrangement for the 10 Totally Ten Grids on Day 100 and then attach the bundle of 10 tens to a narrower hundreds place. The bundle can be fanned out just enough for children to see that 10 Totally Ten Grids make up the hundred.

▶ Play *Collect 100* game. Players will need 200 small counters and 20 ten cups or other containers to hold groups of ten counters. Partners take turns rolling a 4–9 number cube and collecting that number of counters. Whenever ten counters accumulate, they are placed in a ten cup. Players tell their totals before each turn. The first player to reach 100 by filling 10 ten cups wins.

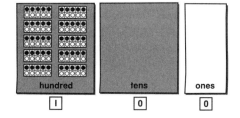

FOCUS

▶ Recognizing, analyzing, and predicting patterns
▶ Knowing the days of the week in order
▶ Counting with one-to-one correspondence
▶ Counting on and counting back
▶ Matching quantities with numerals
▶ Solving problems

MATERIALS

Every Day Calendar, February Month Strip, February Calendar Pieces; or heart and star shapes from Calendar Cutouts (TR21); Today, Yesterday, and Tomorrow Markers (TR21), Calendar Record (TR15)

SUGGESTED PATTERN FOR FEBRUARY

The February Calendar Pieces use red hearts and blue stars to create an ABAB pattern in the order red heart, blue star, red heart, blue star. If you choose to use the hearts and stars from the Calendar Cutouts (TR21), you can use the same or any other pair of colors to create the pattern. Write the dates on the pieces before posting.

The FREQUENCY and UPDATE PROCEDURE for the Calendar continue from November. See page 26 for a detailed description.

DISCUSSION FOR THE SECOND WEEK

Explain that a new pattern is beginning to appear on the February Calendar. Refer to September's Discussion for sample questions (page 8).

There are some special days coming up this month. Involve children in predicting their colors and where they will fall on the Calendar, using the ABAB pattern. Go ahead and place the Calendar Pieces for these days on the Calendar.

▶ Valentine's Day is February 14. What color do you think it will be? How did you get your answer?
▶ Abraham Lincoln's birthday is February 12. Will the piece used on his birthday be the same color as the one on Valentine's Day? How did you decide?
▶ George Washington's birthday is February 22. What color will this piece be? How do you know this?
▶ Presidents' Day, the third Monday of this month, is a national holiday honoring both Presidents' birthdays. Where is the third Monday going to be and what color will it be?

Interpreting the pattern with body motions should be very easy this month, since children will need to think of only two different motions to carry out the alternating ABAB pattern. (See September, page 8.) Let children suggest and try several interpretations for the basic ABAB pattern within one discussion period. At other times, let children use various art materials to create an ABAB pattern of their own. You might ask the class to keep an eye out for ABAB patterns around the school, home, and neighborhood and ask them to tell you when they find one.

DISCUSSION FOR THE END OF THE MONTH

On one of the last days of February, ask children to search the Calendar for some patterns to share with the class. The alternating color pattern will make the pattern of odd and even numbers stand out. The colorful diagonals of the checkerboard pattern may bring out some new number patterns. You might want to record children's observations and any number patterns they point out on a large piece of paper.

HELPFUL HINT

▶ Since the pattern for even numbers is highlighted on the Calendar this month, involve children in brainstorming a list of things that come in 2's. Then, using the list, everyone can suggest story problems that involve counting by 2's. For example, 4 pairs of boots would go on how many feet?

EVERY DAY ELEMENT   BIRTHDAY DATA

FOCUS

▶ Knowing the months of the year in order
▶ Counting, comparing, and ordering small quantities
▶ Counting with one-to-one correspondence to 28
▶ Reading, comparing, and ordering numbers to 28
▶ Solving problems and using mental math
▶ Interpreting organized data

The MATERIALS and FREQUENCY for the Birthday Data continue from September and October. See page 9 and page 18 for a detailed description.

UPDATE PROCEDURE

At the beginning of February, ask the class to point out the Birthday Package that matches the month written above the Calendar. Have the class name all the months in order. Then begin again with January, stopping with a clap on February. Note that February is the second month of the new year.

Feature the February and August Packages near the Calendar if you have decided to recognize summer birthdays on the children's half-year "unbirthdays." (See September Helpful Hints, page 10.) The class can predict where the birthdays and half-year "unbirthdays" will appear on the Calendar and mark them with the tags taken from the Birthday Packages.

DISCUSSION FOR THE BEGINNING OF THE MONTH

See September, page 10 for discussion questions to accompany the identification of the month's birthdays on the Calendar.

DISCUSSION FOR ABRAHAM LINCOLN'S AND GEORGE WASHINGTON'S BIRTHDAYS

Let children know about the upcoming Presidents' Day, honoring the February birthdays of Lincoln and Washington on the 12th and 22nd. (See February Calendar, page 61.) Some teachers have made the Calendar Piece for Presidents' Day stand out by decorating it with an attached quarter and penny.

DISCUSSION DURING THE MONTH

Let the lineup of Birthday Packages provide a focus for some problem solving questions. Fit in a question or two at transition times or when lining up for recess or lunch. For example:

▶ Can you find 2 months that have 5 birthdays in all?
▶ Can you find 2 Birthday Packages that have the same number of tags and together have 6?
▶ Can you find 2 months where one Package has 4 more than the other?

When there is more than one correct solution, you might ask, "Can we find other months where this is also true?" Some days encourage children to provide the clues for the search.

EVERY DAY ELEMENT

COIN COUNTER

FOCUS

▶ Knowing the penny, nickel, dime, and quarter
▶ Knowing the value of each coin and coin equivalencies
▶ Counting by 10's, 5's, and 1's
▶ Determining the value of a collection of coins
▶ Using mental math, including figuring change
▶ Recording money amounts using both the dollar sign and decimal point and the cent sign
▶ Solving problems with coins

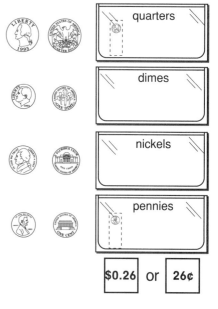

MATERIALS

The MATERIALS for the Coin Counter continue from November and January. See pages 28 and 50 for detailed descriptions. In addition, add a clear pocket labeled *quarters* and the Quarter Demonstration Card to the Coin Counter display. Also, copies of quarter Coin Cards (TR3) or real quarters will be needed.

OVERVIEW

In February, the Coin Counter introduces the quarter. As a penny a day is added to the Counter, children trade 2 dimes and a nickel for a quarter as well as 5 pennies for a nickel and 2 nickels for a dime. Counting out the total value of the coins each day, they get practice in counting on by 10's, 5's, and 1's.

The FREQUENCY and UPDATE PROCEDURE continue from January (see page 50) with the addition of trading the 2 dimes and a nickel for a quarter appearing on the 25th of the month.

DISCUSSION FOR FEBRUARY 25

Identify the quarter's value as 25¢. Add the Quarter Demo Coin and a quarter pocket to the Coin Counter display. Pass around three or four quarters so that each child can feel and briefly examine the real coin. Ask children to look at the quarter and the Large Demo Pictures of all the coins. How is the quarter similar to the other coins? How is it different?

They may mention that the quarter has a man on one side, like the other coins, but that it has a bird on the back. Their observations may give you the opportunity to tell them a little about George Washington, who served from 1789–1797 as the nation's first President. You could identify the bird on the back as an eagle and explain that *E pluribus unum* means "out of many, one," referring to the creation of the United States out of the several colonies. Following the discussion, collect the quarters and use one in the Update Procedure to replace the two dimes and the nickel.

DISCUSSION DURING THE MONTH

Asking some of the following questions now and then during the month may help develop children's mental math:

▶   How many coins are in our Counter?

▶   Can you think of a different group of coins we could use that would add up to the same amount?

▶   What coins do you think will be in our Counter on the 8th? On the 11th? On the 17th? On the 20th?

▶   If you were to take today's money from the Coin Counter to the store, would you have enough to buy something for 12¢? 15¢? 25¢? If so, would you get change? How much?

Sometimes invite children to suggest store problems of their own.

HELPFUL HINTS

▶   February is a most appropriate month for introducing the quarter. Some teachers note Washington's and Lincoln's birthdays on the Calendar by attaching a quarter or a Quarter Coin Card on February 22, a penny on February 12, or both coins on Presidents' Day. (See February Birthday Data, page 63.)

▶   Play *Coin Collector* game, using real coins. Partners take turns tossing a 1–6 number cube and collecting that amount in pennies. Five pennies are traded for a nickel whenever possible, and two nickels are traded for a dime whenever possible. Players state their total amounts before each toss. The first player to trade two dimes and a nickel for a quarter is the winner.

▶   Reading and displaying a few picture books that describe the Revolutionary War period and George Washington's life may spark children's interest in American History.

FOCUS

▶ Understanding processes of addition and subtraction

▶ Using the language of addition and subtraction and comparison

▶ Discussing part and whole relationships for the sets of 10

▶ Seeing patterns in addition and subtraction

▶ Using symbolic notation to record addition and subtraction

▶ Matching quantities and numerals

▶ Understanding place value

▶ Sharing number stories to relate two small quantities to each other

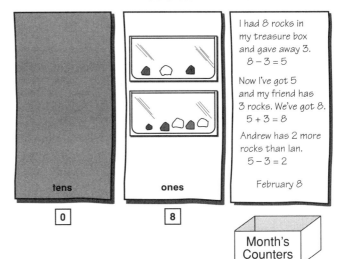

I had 8 rocks in my treasure box and gave away 3.
$8 - 3 = 5$

Now I've got 5 and my friend has 3 rocks. We've got 8.
$5 + 3 = 8$

Andrew has 2 more rocks than Ian.
$5 - 3 = 2$

February 8

Month's Counters

MATERIALS

The Depositor (from November), 29 rocks, shells, or other counters

The FREQUENCY and UPDATE PROCEDURE continue from November. See page 32 for a detailed description. This month allow for extended discussion when combinations for 7 and 8 appear on the ones side (on February 7, 8, 17, 18, 27, and 28).

DISCUSSION DURING THE MONTH

On the days when 7 or 8 counters have been placed in the 2 clear pockets on the ones side, encourage children to share number stories. Record each with a few words and a number sentence on large paper nearby. Help children read the number sentence aloud in a way that relates to the story that was told. For example, on February 8, with 5 in one pocket and 3 in the other, a child might offer, "I have 5 rocks and my friend has 3. Together we have 8." Then the number sentence, $5 + 3 = 8$, could be read back, "Five and three made eight in all." If the child gave this same story but concluded with, "I have 2 more rocks than my friend," the comparison would be with a subtraction sentence $5 - 3 = 2$. This could be read back, "Five matched up with three shows two extras," or, "Five compared to three gives a difference of two." Yet another interpretation could be, "I had 8 rocks and gave 3 to my friend, so now I have 5," which would result in $8 - 3 = 5$. This could be read back, "Eight take away or give away three leaves five."

When a few stories for the day's combination have been shared, you might take the counters out of the pockets. Ask for volunteers to place them into the pockets in a different way. After recording and reading back the number sentence for each volunteer's story, ask, "Does someone have a story idea for putting the counters into the pockets in another way that we haven't yet seen?" The resulting stories and number sentences will expose children to a variety of combinations for the numbers.

FOCUS
▶ Collecting and recording data on a graph over time
▶ Reading and interpreting data on a picture or bar graph
▶ Organizing quantities into pairs and counting by 2's
▶ Recognizing odd and even patterns

MATERIALS
Every Day Graph (TR9), 29 shoe markers (TR12)

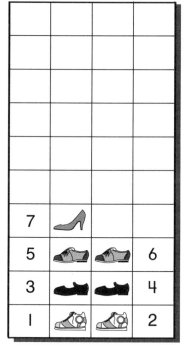

Odd   Even

OVERVIEW
This month the Graph will display odd and even quantities and encourage counting by 2's. When one shoe picture is added each day, pairs form on the second, fourth, sixth, eighth, and so on, helping children see that an even number of objects can be broken into pairs. On the odd-numbered days, the collection of shoes shows an extra shoe with no partner.

FREQUENCY
Update daily and discuss once a week.

UPDATE PROCEDURE
Beginning on the first of the month, add a picture of a shoe each day, forming a pair every 2 days. On Mondays, add shoes for Saturday, Sunday, and Monday. Ask the class to count all the pairs by 2's, counting on the extra one on odd-numbered days. Ask if the day's number of shoes reveals an even "all paired up" arrangement or an odd arrangement showing an extra shoe with no partner. Record the total each day next to the last shoe.

DISCUSSION DURING THE MONTH
Once a week, following the Update Procedure, focus discussion on the emerging odd/even pattern. Questions to foster conversation might include:
▶ How can you tell if the number is even or odd? What does it mean to be an odd or an even number?
▶ How many more days until the number of shoes will be even again? Odd again?
▶ Can we find a pattern in the even numbers we have written so far? In the odd numbers?
▶ If I mark the last day of February on the Graph with an *x*, can you look at the pattern and decide if the last day will be even or odd? How do you know?
▶ How many shoes will there be on the last day of the month?

Helpful Hints

▶ Ask the class to look for connections between the ABAB patterns emerging on the Calendar and the Shoe Graph.

▶ Whenever the opportunity arises during the month, try counting quantities by 2's instead of always by 1's. For example, it might be fun to take attendance counting those present by 2's. Is the total odd or even? If we pair up with partners today, will someone be left without a partner?

▶ One teacher at Newman School in New Orleans records the children's responses to, "What does it mean to be an odd number or an even number?" One child's comment, "Being an odd number is not having a partner to dance with," inspired the beginning of an illustrated odd-and-even book.

▶ Exploring odd and even numbers can be done easily on the calculator. Let children add 1 and 2 to various numbers of their choice. Discuss what they notice.

MARCH

MORE TO THINK ABOUT

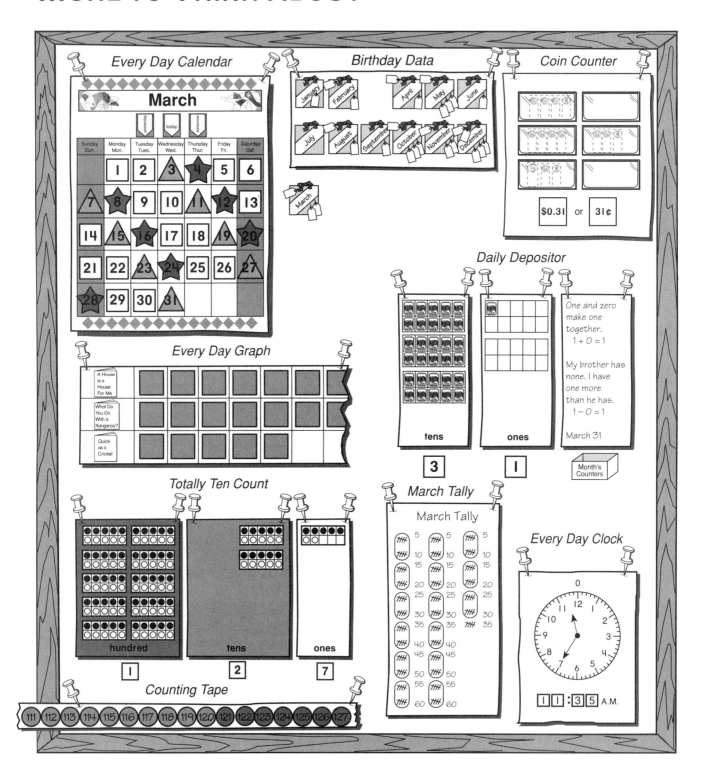

Every Day Calendar

March

Birthday Data

Coin Counter

$0.31 or 31¢

Every Day Graph

Daily Depositor

One and zero make one together.
1 + O = 1

My brother has none. I have one more than he has.
1 − O = 1

March 31

tens ones

3 1

Month's Counters

Totally Ten Count

hundred tens ones

1 2 7

March Tally

Every Day Clock

11:35 A.M.

Counting Tape

111 112 113 114 115 116 117 118 119 120 121 122 123 124 125 126 127

This month the Counting Tape and Totally Ten Count familiarize children with quantities above 100. Children see relationships and make connections at different times. For example, while some can see "tens" and "ones" on the Counting Tape from the 11th day of school, others may not make the connection until focusing on the Tape for several months, and some not until year's end. An attitude of joy at their insights encourages even children with the least sophisticated number sense to get involved.

The Calendar takes on a new look with the use of Calendar Pieces which vary in shape as well as color. Children practice identifying squares and triangles. Birthday Data offers more problem solving with small numbers.

The Coin Counter and the Clock will each be used in new ways in March. The Coin Counter displays up to three suggested arrangements of coins equal to the day's date in cents. The Clock features reading the hour and minute hands together, counting minutes past the hour in 5's and 1's.

The Daily Depositor loses its clear pockets (to the Coin Counter) and collects canceled stamps on 2" × 5" grids instead. These arrays of 10 stamps become the first pages of a "Collector's Album" at month's end. The Graph is the highlight of March. Children love to be asked their opinions and to have them recorded. This month the class decides on a survey question, conducts a poll, graphs part of the sample each day, and analyzes the accumulating data. The class survey may encourage some children to do polls of their own.

EVERY DAY ELEMENT   COUNTING TAPE

FOCUS

▶ Developing number sense
▶ Counting with one-to-one correspondence
▶ Grouping and counting by 10's and 1's
▶ Understanding place value
▶ Comparing and ordering quantities
▶ Counting on and counting back
▶ Extending number patterns and using mental math
▶ Solving problems

The MATERIALS, FREQUENCY, and UPDATE PROCEDURE for the Counting Tape continue from September. See pages 2 and 3 for a detailed description. Repeat the same sequence of colors used for the decades to 100 when putting up shapes for Days 101–110, 111–120, 121–130, 131–140, and so on.

Teacher: What number will we write on today's Counting Tape?

Class: We will write 120.

Teacher: Would someone be willing to share how you decided it would be the 120th day of school?

Child: Yesterday was 119, so today is 120.

Teacher: So you used the counting pattern to figure out that the next number would be 120. Let's say the pattern, beginning with the first day after Day 100.

Class: 101, 102, 103 . . . 120.

Teacher: The colors from Day 101 to Day 120 match the colors of two groups of ten somewhere else on the Counting Tape. Can you find them?

Child: The first 2 tens.

Teacher: Yes, 1 to 20 are the same colors as 101 to 120. Let's count the circles after Day 100 by tens.

Class: 110, 120.

Teacher: Tell me how to write today's number on today's circle.

Class: One hundred, 2 tens, and 0 ones; 120.

Teacher: Yes, the 1 is for the first 100, the 2 is for the 2 tens after 100, and the 0 is for no ones. Finally, can you figure out how many groups of ten you have all together in 120?

Child: Ten tens to 100 and 2 more; 12 groups of 10.

Continue to include questions that encourage counting on, counting back, adding, and comparing. (See September, pages 3 and 4.) This will help children see that the relationships between numbers above 100 are the same as for the numbers to 100.

EVERY DAY ELEMENT

CLOCK

FOCUS

▶ Experiencing duration
▶ Understanding analog and digital clocks
▶ Learning how many minutes in an hour
▶ Counting by 5's and 1's
▶ Reading the minute and hour hands

The MATERIALS and FREQUENCY for the Clock continue from January. See page 46 for a detailed description.

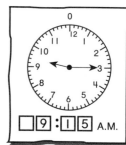
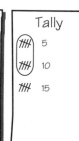

OVERVIEW

In March, the Clock advances just 5 minutes each day of the month.

UPDATE PROCEDURE

Begin with the hands of the Clock showing 9:00 A.M. Each day advance the hands of the Clock ahead 5 minutes, having the class count each minute. On the first of March, the hands will stop at 9:05 A.M.; on the second, 9:10 A.M. Finally, record the time in digital form below the Every Day Clock and read it together.

On the 13th of the month, discontinue the use of the Clock or begin another journey around advancing the hands to 10:05 A.M.

DISCUSSION DURING THE MONTH

Children often have difficulty with language that describes duration. Frequently asking a question or two similar to those that follow may help children become more familiar with these often confusing terms.

▶ What time is it right now?

▶ What time will it be 2 minutes from now?

▶ What time will it be 5 minutes after the present time?

▶ In 10 minutes, we'll be going to recess. What time will that be?

▶ What time was it 5 minutes ago?

▶ How many minutes have passed since 9:00?

HELPFUL HINTS

▶ To encourage children to use their clock-reading skills to interpret the hands on the classroom clock, invite them to raise their hand when they "catch" the classroom clock showing the time that matches the time shown on the Every Day Clock for the day.

▶ Some teachers show how to mark a tally of 5 each day on a paper near the Clock, giving children another experience counting by 5's.

▶ To let children explore counting by 5's, show them how to use the constant feature of their calculators.
(Press ⊞ 5 ⟌ ⟌ ⟌ . . . .)

EVERY DAY ELEMENT

TOTALLY TEN COUNT

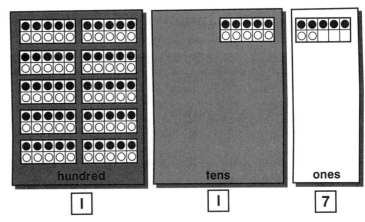

FOCUS

▶ Developing number sense

▶ Grouping and counting by 10's, 5's, and 1's

▶ Understanding place value

▶ Learning addition combinations for sums 5 through 10

▶ Adding or subtracting 10 and 100 using place value models

▶ Using mental math

The MATERIALS and FREQUENCY for the Totally Ten Count continue from November. See page 25 for a detailed description.

UPDATE PROCEDURE

The recently-completed 100 in the hundreds place provides a model to help children understand the meaning of the digits in three-place numbers. When recording the day's total number of dots, ask children to tell you what digit to write under each place and what it means. For example, on Day 117, "1 hundred, 1 ten, and 7 ones; 117."

DISCUSSION DURING THE MONTH

As in November (see page 25), continue to talk about the addition combinations for 5 and 10 appearing in the Grid on the ones side.

To encourage thinking in hundreds, tens, and ones, you might occasionally ask, "How much would we have if we added another hundred? Or another ten? Or another single dot?"

EVERY DAY ELEMENT

CALENDAR

FOCUS
▶ Recognizing, analyzing, and predicting patterns
▶ Knowing the days of the week in order
▶ Counting with one-to-one correspondence
▶ Counting on and counting back
▶ Matching quantities with numerals
▶ Solving problems

MATERIALS
Every Day Calendar, March Month Strip, March Calendar Pieces; or square, triangle, and star shapes from Calendar Cutouts (TR21); Today, Yesterday, and Tomorrow Markers (TR21), Calendar Record (TR15)

SUGGESTED PATTERN FOR MARCH
The March Calendar Pieces use orange squares, green triangles, and blue stars to create an AABC pattern in the order orange square, orange square, green triangle, blue star. If you choose to use the square, triangle, and star shapes from the Calendar Cutouts (TR21), you can use the same or any other set of three colors to create the pattern. Write the dates on the pieces before posting.

The FREQUENCY and UPDATE PROCEDURE for the Calendar continue from November. See page 26 for a detailed description.

DISCUSSION AT THE END OF THE SECOND WEEK
Explain that a new pattern is beginning to appear on the March Calendar. Refer to September's Discussion for sample questions.

Interpreting the pattern with body motions may again be difficult for some children, since they will need to use three different motions to create an AABC pattern. (See September, page 8.) Allow children to try several interpretations for the basic AABC pattern within one discussion period. At other times, let children use various art materials or manipulatives to create an AABC pattern of their own.

DISCUSSION FOR THE END OF THE MONTH
On one of the last days of March, ask children to look for some patterns on the Calendar to share with the class. (The color pattern will highlight several diagonals in which the numbers increase by 8 going downward to the right.) The multiples of 4 will also stand out. You might record children's observations and any number patterns they point out on a large piece of paper.

The stars go down 4, 12, 20 and 8, 16, 24.
The pattern is orange, orange, green, blue, orange, orange, green, blue.
It goes square, square, triangle, star.
The blue stars go 4, 8, 12, 16, 20, 24, 28....
The green triangles go down the stairs.
It's four from one star to the next star.
All the squares have a partner square.
The green ones go down by 8's.

HELPFUL HINTS

▶ Since counting by 4's will be highlighted on this month's calendar color pattern, it might be fun to brainstorm a list of things that come in 4's. These can be used in story problems that encourage children to add 4 at a time. For example: How many wheels are on one car? Two cars? Three cars? If 4 quarters are worth 1 dollar, how many quarters can I get for 2 dollars? If some cookies come four to a package, how many cookies will I have if I buy two packages? Three packages? Four?

▶ Remind children how to use the constant feature of their calculators and let them verify their answers.

EVERY DAY ELEMENT   BIRTHDAY DATA

FOCUS

▶ Knowing the months of the year in order
▶ Counting, comparing, and ordering small quantities
▶ Counting with one-to-one correspondence to 31
▶ Reading, comparing, and ordering numbers to 31
▶ Solving problems with mental math
▶ Interpreting organized data

The MATERIALS, FREQUENCY, and UPDATE PROCEDURE for the Birthday Data continue from September and October. See page 9 and page 18 for a detailed description.

DISCUSSION DURING THE MONTH

Occasionally, ask children to figure how many days until the next birthday. How much older is one March birthday child than another? Listen to those willing to share how they came to their conclusions. The lineup of Birthday Packages continues to offer an ever-present invitation to compare, count, add, and subtract. A few examples of the kinds of questions that get children thinking follow:

▶ Are there more birthdays this month or during your birthday month?
▶ How many birthdays come in March and April? In April and May?
▶ How many months until your birthday month arrives?
▶ How many fewer birthdays are in January than in April?
▶ I see 2 months next to each other where the tags add up to 6 in all. Which 2 months could these be?

When there is more than one possible correct answer, acknowledge one solution, then ask for another.

EVERY DAY ELEMENT

COIN COUNTER

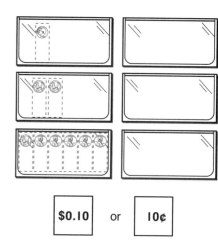

FOCUS

▶ Knowing the penny, nickel, dime, and quarter
▶ Knowing the value of each coin and coin equivalencies
▶ Counting by 10's, 5's, and 1's
▶ Adding mixed coins
▶ Using mental math, including figuring change
▶ Recording money amounts using both the dollar sign and decimal point and the cent sign
▶ Solving problems with coins

MATERIALS

Coin Cards (TR3), 3 rows of 2 small 3" × 6" clear pockets, Demo Coins (TR17–20)(optional)

OVERVIEW

Since it was introduced in November, the Coin Counter has been used to gradually build children's confidence in recognizing and adding combinations of coins. The exchanges of pennies for a nickel, and nickels for a dime, have made children aware that an amount can be represented with more than one set of coins.

Beginning this month, children will be asked to think up and display in the Counter different combinations of coins whose value equals the day's date. This gives the Coin Counter a problem-solving focus. As children check the total value of the proposed coin combinations placed in the Counter, they gain additional practice counting mixed coins.

FREQUENCY

Update daily and discuss once a week.

UPDATE PROCEDURE

Ask the class to think of a coin or coins which would add up to the day's date in cents. On the first through the fourth of the month, children will be able to suggest only one way, using pennies. On the fifth through the ninth, they may come up with two ways. From the tenth on, they may think up several combinations of coins.

Ask children to place each combination of coins into one row of the Counter in order of decreasing value from left to right. Have the class check each set of coins placed in the Counter by counting up the total value in unison. Finally, record the total for the day in both the dollar sign and decimal point and the cent sign forms below the Counter. At the day's end, empty the pockets.

DISCUSSION DURING THE MONTH

Once a week, after children's suggestion of coins for the day are displayed in the Counter, ask them to decide which pocket holds the least coins and to think of a way to make the day's date using even fewer coins. Is it possible, or is the solution with the fewest coins already displayed in the Counter?

Now and then ask children to imagine using the coins shown in the Counter to make some small purchases. For example:

▶ If you take the coins from one row of today's Counter to the store, will you have enough to buy something for 12¢?

▶ If so, which coins could you give the clerk?

▶ If not, how much more money would you need?

Occasionally invite children to contribute store problems of their own.

EVERY DAY ELEMENT

DAILY DEPOSITOR AND NUMBER STORIES

FOCUS

▶ Understanding processes of addition and subtraction

▶ Using the language of addition and subtraction and comparison

▶ Discussing part and whole relationships for the sets to 10

▶ Seeing patterns in addition and subtraction

▶ Using symbolic notation to record addition and subtraction

▶ Matching quantities and numerals

▶ Understanding place value

▶ Sharing number stories to relate two small quantities to each other

I had 5 stamps and got 4 more.
$$5 + 4 = 9$$
Five is one more than four.
$$5 - 4 = 1$$
Andrea had 9, but she gave 4 away. Now she has 5.
$$9 - 4 = 5$$
March 5

Month's Counters

MATERIALS

Adapt the Depositor, assembled in November, by removing the small clear pockets and replacing them with two 2" × 5" grids made from Inch Squared Paper (TR11). Continue to use the Depositor with a new collection of counters, for example, 31 canceled postage stamps.

FREQUENCY

Update daily and allow for extended discussion when combinations for 8, 9, or 10 appear on the ones side (March 8, 9, 10, 18, 19, 20, 28, 29, 30).

UPDATE PROCEDURE

This will vary from past months in two ways. Instead of placing each day's stamp into a pocket, use a paper clip or tape to attach it to one of the two grids on the ones side. Then whenever these stamps add up to ten, move the stamps from one grid to fill the empty spaces on the second grid. The completed grid of ten stamps then moves to the tens side of the Depositor. Record the day's total tens and ones below the Depositor. Allow the class to propose one or two stories to go with the arrangement of the day's counters. Record a related number sentence and help the class read it using both everyday language and math language.

DISCUSSION DURING THE MONTH

On the days when 8, 9, or 10 stamps have been attached to the grids on the ones side, allow children to share several stories and record each with a few words and a number sentence on a large piece of paper nearby. Help children read the number sentence back in a way that relates to the story that was told. For example, on March 9, with 5 in the top grid and 4 below, a child might offer, "I had 5 stamps and got 4 more. Then I had 9." Then the number sentence 5 + 4 = 9 could be read back, "5 and 4 makes 9 in all." If the child gave a story such as, "I have one more stamp than my friend," the comparison would be recorded with a subtraction sentence, 5 − 4 = 1. This could be read back, "5 matched up with 4 shows 1 extra." Another story could be, "I had 9 stamps and gave 4 to my friend, so now I have 5," which would result in 9 − 4 = 5. This could be read, "9 take away 4 leaves 5."

To expose children to a variety of combinations for 8, 9, and 10, investigate how many ways the stamps can be placed onto the grids. (See February, page 65.)

ones

9

I had 5 stamps and got 4 more.
5 + 4 = 9
Five is one more than four.
5 − 4 = 1
Andrea had 9, but she gave 4 away. Now she has 5.
9 − 4 = 5

HELPFUL HINTS

▶ Children love to examine the canceled postage stamps and share some of the things they notice, in much the same way as they enjoyed studying coins. You might pass out a stamp to each child and invite several to tell about some features they notice. Then pick one of the characteristics mentioned by a child and sort the stamps into two groups—those that have the named attribute and those that do not. Finally predict and confirm which group has more and which has less. Sometimes the piles will be close enough in quantity to require counting them or lining the groups up in one-to-one correspondence.

▶ At the end of the month, the filled grids can form the pages of a class stamp album. Most children enjoy contributing and keeping track of the growing collection throughout the year.

12 with people.   <   14 with no people.

FOCUS

▶ Collecting and recording data on a graph
▶ Reading and interpreting data on a bar graph
▶ Counting and comparing small quantities
▶ Sampling and generalizing

MATERIALS

Every Day Graph (TR9), several $1\frac{3}{4}$" square paper markers in a bright color

OVERVIEW

In March, we suggest using the Every Day Graph to display the results of a preference poll or class survey. Children enjoy sharing their opinions. The following are examples of questions often posed to children when graphing their interests:

▶ Which of these pets would you most like to have?
▶ Would you prefer to eat a chocolate, vanilla, or strawberry ice cream cone?
▶ Which of these four colors do you like the best?
▶ Which of these four outdoor activities would you enjoy doing most?
▶ Which of these three school activities do you enjoy the most?
▶ Which of these three stories did you enjoy the most?

It is this last suggestion of a "Favorite Book" Graph that we have chosen to use as an example of a preference poll for March. But any question you or the children choose will produce data and a graph your class will be interested in analyzing.

FREQUENCY

Create the Graph over the period of one week. Discuss several times during that week and later in the month.

UPDATE PROCEDURE

During the initial survey and creation of a class graph (see Discussion that follows), each child prepares a colored marker that indicates his or her preference. All markers are put into a sack. For several days, have volunteers pull four or five markers at random out of the class's collection and attach them to the Graph, so it grows slowly.

Each time more children's opinions are represented on the Graph, a more complete picture of the entire class's preferences becomes apparent. Ask children each day if the new data changes their thinking about what the entire Graph will look like when everyone's marker is up. Does the choice that had the most markers yesterday still have the most or has a different choice taken the lead? Do we have enough markers up yet to predict which choice will be ahead when the whole class sample is graphed?

DISCUSSION ON THE DAY OF POLLING THE CLASS AND CREATING THE GRAPH

Pose a survey question (chosen by you or the class) to the children. Ask them to copy down their choice from the possible answers (without consulting others) onto their own graphing marker. (See Materials.) They do not need to put their names on the markers. Anonymity tends to make children respond more freely without worrying about what others will think of their choice. Let the class know there are no right or wrong answers. If more people prefer strawberry ice cream, it doesn't make it the right choice for you if chocolate is your favorite. We can make our own choices true to our own feelings. Don't forget to include yourself. Collect the markers and put them in a sack or a box.

Then involve the class in constructing the Graph, deciding how to cut and tape copies of the Every Day Graph (TR9) to create a grid suited to the data collected. How many rows do we need for the categories? Can we predict how many spaces we'll need for the longest row? What is the most we could need? Is it likely that we'll need that many? After the grid has been assembled, mix up the markers and pull out 5 or 6 at random to attach to the Graph. What does this data show? Ask children if they think they can predict by looking at this first bit of data which choice will be ahead when all the markers are up. Let a few children share their thinking. Each day thereafter have a volunteer update the Graph with more data. (See Update Procedure.)

DISCUSSION WHEN ALL THE MARKERS HAVE BEEN GRAPHED

When the Graph finally represents everyone's choices, focus the class on interpreting the data. You could ask, "What does our Graph tell us?" or "What do we know about our class's choices from the Graph?" Fill in, if necessary, with some questions that help them see which choices were made by the most, and which by the fewest, students. This is a good time, perhaps, to remind them that the less popular choices were just as right for the people who made them as the one made by the most students. Having different ideas and opinions make our class interesting. Sometimes children who made a choice not shared by many of their classmates appreciate some reassurance, even when there are no names on the markers.

Some questions could include:
► Was one choice made by a lot more people or did the choice with the most only have a few more people who chose it?
► How many people's opinions are shown on our Graph?
► How many markers are on our Graph in all? Could someone share how you got your total?
► Did we think our Graph would turn out like this when it only had ten markers? Were ten markers enough for us to make a smart prediction?

HELPFUL HINTS

▶ When asking questions about a graph, it is helpful to provide a "thinking time" for children who need some time to reflect without being influenced by the quick responders. During these few seconds of "thinking time," no one is allowed to call out answers. After this quiet time, some teachers say, "Class," as a signal that anyone who wants to answer can join in for a group response. This is an easy way to become aware of the level of confidence in the class and the proportion of correct and incorrect answers. Some children who are not inclined to raise their hands and offer their thinking when everyone's attention is on them are more likely to respond as part of a group. For questions with correct answers, the focus can switch from the answers to the strategies different class members use to get their answers. Asking frequently, "Would someone be willing to share how they got _____ for an answer?" helps everyone see different ways of approaching the question. Building this kind of sharing into class discussions helps children see strategies they might not have used and helps them become better communicators.

▶ Children often enjoy doing surveys of their own. Allow children to decide on their own survey questions and to carry clipboards around, polling their classmates during a "choosing time" work period. Limiting the class to two pollsters on any one day keeps interruptions of the other children's pursuits to a minimum. Most classmates enjoy being asked to give their opinion or preference and having someone care enough to mark it down. The different polls form a display of considerable interest to the group—so many comparisons to make and so much to talk about!

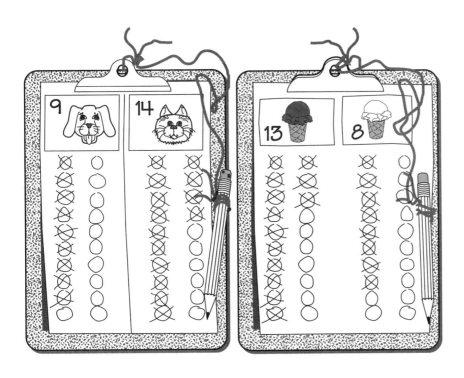

APRIL

SPRING INTO THE MONTH

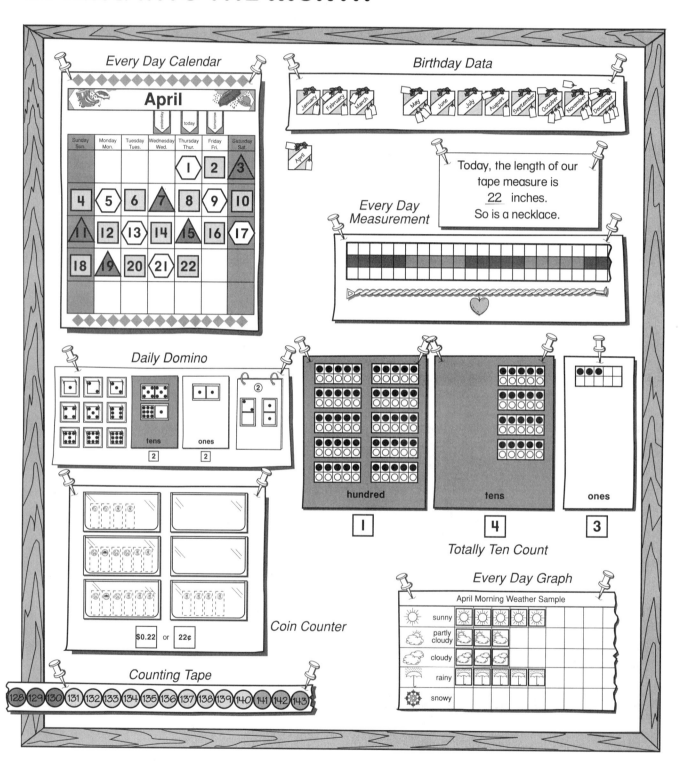

Every Day Calendar

April

Birthday Data

Today, the length of our tape measure is __22__ inches. So is a necklace.

Every Day Measurement

Daily Domino

tens 2   ones 2

hundred 1   tens 4   ones 3

Totally Ten Count

Coin Counter

$0.22 or 22¢

Every Day Graph

April Morning Weather Sample

sunny							
partly cloudy							
cloudy							
rainy							
snowy							

Counting Tape

128 129 130 131 132 133 134 135 136 137 138 139 140 141 142 143

In April, the Clock is replaced with a new Measurement element, which focuses on estimating and measuring length in inches. The Depositor is transformed into a new Daily Domino element. The Graph keeps track of the spring weather, providing a sample to compare with fall and winter data.

The Counting Tape and Totally Ten Count continue with their progression of three-place numbers. The Calendar and Birthday Data offer more experiences with patterns and problem solving.

EVERY DAY ELEMENT

COUNTING TAPE

FOCUS

▶ Developing number sense
▶ Counting with one-to-one correspondence
▶ Grouping and counting by 10's and 1's
▶ Understanding place value
▶ Comparing and ordering quantities
▶ Counting on and counting back
▶ Extending number patterns and using mental math
▶ Solving problems

The MATERIALS, FREQUENCY, and UPDATE PROCEDURE for the Counting Tape continue from September. See pages 2 and 3 for a detailed description. Continue to repeat the same sequence of colors used for the groups of ten up to 100 when putting up shapes for Days 101–110, 111–120, 121–130, 131–140, and so on.

DISCUSSION DURING THE MONTH

Continue to focus on ways that the counting pattern for numbers above 100 is like the sequence up to 100. For example, Day 143 follows Day 142 just as Day 43 followed Day 42. See March, page 70 for discussion suggestions. To foster number sense, continue to include questions that encourage counting on, counting back, comparing, and adding and subtracting. See September, pages 3 and 4 for examples of these kinds of questions.

HELPFUL HINTS

▶ If Day 150 arrives in April, take the time to talk about 50 being one half of 100. (See November's Day 50 Discussion on page 24.) Encourage children to estimate where Day 200 might come on the Counting Tape if school were to last until then.

▶ Counting by 1's is an opportunity to let children explore patterns with larger numbers on their calculators. Suggest that they enter a number—63, for example—and add 1. Then enter 163 and add 1. Let them continue with numbers of their choice. Discuss what they see.

FOCUS

▶ Developing number sense
▶ Grouping and counting by 10's, 5's, and 1's
▶ Understanding place value
▶ Learning addition combinations for sums 5 through 10
▶ Adding or subtracting 10 and 100 using place value models
▶ Using mental math

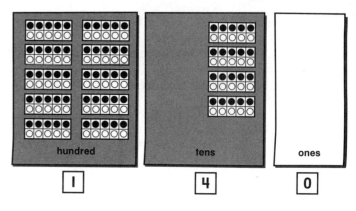

hundred | tens | ones

| 1 | 4 | 0 |

The MATERIALS and FREQUENCY for the Totally Ten Count continue from November. See page 25 for a detailed description.

UPDATE PROCEDURE

As in March (see page 71), continue to have the class tell what digit to write under each place and what it means. For example, on Day 140, count "1 hundred, 4 tens, and 0 ones."

DISCUSSION DURING THE MONTH

Continue talking about the addition combinations for 5 and 10 appearing in the Grid on the ones side and practice adding and subtracting 10's in the tens place. See November, page 25, for possible questioning strategies.

To encourage children thinking in 100's, 10's, and 1's, occasionally ask them, "How much would we have if we added another hundred? Or another ten? Or another single dot?"

HELPFUL HINT

▶ If you need display space for the new Daily Domino and Measuring activities in April, consider retiring the Totally Ten Count for the rest of the year. Its main goal, exposing children to three-place numbers and the counting pattern above 100, has been met.

FOCUS

▶ Recognizing, analyzing, and predicting patterns
▶ Knowing the days of the week in order
▶ Counting with one-to-one correspondence
▶ Counting on and counting back
▶ Matching quantities with numerals
▶ Solving problems

MATERIALS

Every Day Calendar, April Month Strip, April Calendar Pieces; or hexagon, square, and triangle shapes from Calendar Cutouts (TR21); Today, Yesterday, and Tomorrow Markers (TR21), Calendar Record (TR15)

SUGGESTED PATTERN FOR APRIL

The April Calendar Pieces use yellow hexagons, orange squares, and green triangles to create an ABCB pattern in the order yellow hexagon, orange square, green triangle, orange square. If you choose to use the hexagon, square, and triangle shapes from the Calendar Cutouts (TR21), you can use the same or any other set of three colors to create the pattern. Write the dates on the pieces before posting.

The FREQUENCY and UPDATE PROCEDURE for the Calendar continue from November. See page 26 for a detailed description.

DISCUSSION FOR THE END OF THE SECOND WEEK

A new pattern appears on the April Calendar. Refer to September's Discussion for sample questions (page 8).

In addition to asking children to predict the next day's piece, we can ask them to determine the color and shape of the piece that will appear in one week, two weeks, or on the last day of the month. This encourages a variety of counting on and mental math strategies. Some children will count all the spaces to the designated space. Others will count full weeks as seven and will use the columns on the Calendar to quicky locate the space. Invite children to share how they came up with their predictions of the shape and color so the group can see several approaches. Ask children to make predictions two or three more times during the month to give them a chance to use their strategies again or to try out someone else's the next time.

Continue to encourage children to suggest and try different ideas for acting out the pattern, assigning different body motions to the A, B, and C. (See September, page 8.) At other times, have children use various art materials, collections, or other manipulatives to create a version of the month's ABCB pattern on their own.

DISCUSSION FOR THE END OF THE MONTH

On one of the last days of April, ask children to look for some patterns to point out to the class. The color pattern will make several diagonals stand out. The multiples of 2 will all be the same color, providing exposure once again to the pattern of even numbers. You might want to record children's comments and any number patterns they point out on a large piece of paper.

The pattern goes yellow, orange, green, orange over and over.
All the even numbers are orange.
The squares go 2, 4, 6, 8, 10, 12, 14, 16, 18, 20 . . .
The yellow hexagons go down 5, 13, 21, 29 . . .
The squares go down like a staircase either way.
The triangles go down 7, 15, 23, and 11, 19, 27 . . .

HELPFUL HINT

▶ Since counting by 2's is highlighted in this month's Calendar pattern, review the list created in February of things that come in 2's, or brainstorm a new list. These suggestions can be used in story problems that encourage children to add by 2's. For example:

How many wheels are on two bikes? Three bikes? Four bikes?

How many mittens are in one pair? Two pairs? Three pairs?

If I get two nickels for one dime, how many can I get for two dimes? Three dimes? Four dimes?

If I cut a muffin in half, I'd get two pieces. How many pieces will I get if I cut two muffins in half?

If it takes two people to turn one jump rope, how many people do we need to turn three ropes? Four ropes?

EVERY DAY ELEMENT   BIRTHDAY DATA

FOCUS

▶ Knowing the months of the year in order
▶ Counting, comparing, and ordering small quantities
▶ Counting with one-to-one correspondence to 30
▶ Reading, comparing, and ordering numbers to 30
▶ Solving problems and using mental math
▶ Interpreting organized data

The MATERIALS, FREQUENCY, and UPDATE PROCEDURE for the Birthday Data continue from September and October. See page 9 and page 18 for a detailed description.

DISCUSSION FOR THE BEGINNING OF THE MONTH

See September, page 10, for discussion questions to accompany the identification of the month's birthdays on the Calendar.

DISCUSSION DURING THE MONTH

Ask questions that involve children in adding and comparing the sets of tags on the different packages. For example:

▶ I see a month that has four more birthdays than January has. Which month could this be?

▶ I see two months that have seven birthdays in all. One month has one fewer birthday than the other month. What are the two months?

When there is more than one possible solution, ask children to search for other possibilities.

EVERY DAY ELEMENT

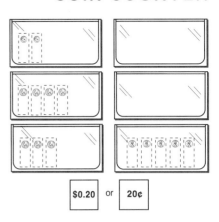

FOCUS

▶ Knowing the penny, nickel, dime, and quarter
▶ Knowing the value of each coin and coin equivalencies
▶ Counting by 10's, 5's, and 1's
▶ Determining the value of a collection of coins
▶ Using mental math, including figuring change
▶ Recording money amounts using both the dollar sign and decimal point and the cent sign
▶ Solving problems with coins

The MATERIALS, FREQUENCY, and UPDATE PROCEDURE for the Coin Counter continue from March. See page 74 for a detailed description. The Coin Counter displays up to three different combinations of coins, each equal to the day's date in cents.

DISCUSSION DURING THE MONTH

Once a week, after children's suggestions of coins for the day are displayed in the Coin Counter, ask them to decide which pocket holds the fewest coins. Also ask them to think of a way to make the day's date using even fewer coins. Is it possible, or is the solution with the fewest coins already displayed in the Coin Counter?

Occasionally, ask children to imagine using the coins shown in the Counter to make some small purchases. For example:
▶ If you were to take the coins from one row of today's Coin Counter to the store, would you have enough to buy something for 15¢? If so, which coins would you give the clerk? If not, how much more money would you need?

Children may enjoy suggesting store problems of their own.

HELPFUL HINTS

▶ Gather a "play store" collection of a few objects labeled with prices to 40¢. A volunteer draws one item out of the store box and the class decides (depending on its price) which coins to use to purchase it.

▶ This is an opportunity for children to use calculators. If children make purchases without the exact amount, they can use a calculator to check whether they got the correct change.

FOCUS

▶ Seeing part and whole relationships
▶ Working with addition combinations to 10
▶ Solving problems

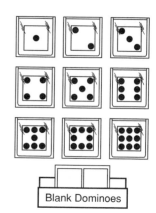

MATERIALS

The Depositor tens- and ones-place papers without the small clear pockets (see March, page 75), 2 laminated cards for recording tens and ones, 9 library pockets holding Domino Halves cut from 8 copies of TR6, a pocket holding Double Domino Blanks cut from 6 copies of TR5, ten 9" × 12" pieces of construction paper labeled 1 through 10

OVERVIEW

The Daily Domino takes the place of the Daily Depositor in April, May, and June. As with the Depositor (see November, pages 31 and 32), children work with combinations to 10. They create a "domino" to place on the ones side of the Depositor each day. On the 10th, the domino with 10 dots moves to the tens place. Prior to assembling the new day's domino, the domino on the ones side from the day before is removed and placed on a piece of construction paper labeled with its sum. These construction paper sheets numbered 1 through 10 provide a display of all the different dominoes created throughout the month. Children work to find as many different combinations as possible by the month's end, trying not to use the same combination twice. The display of dominoes, organized by sums, provides review of all the addition "fact families" to 10. The dominoes can also be used to practice "missing addend" subtraction. This occurs when children are asked to figure out how many dots are hidden when shown only one half of a domino.

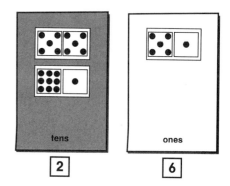

FREQUENCY

Update daily with a brief discussion. On Monday, construct dominoes for Saturday and Sunday to add to the month's collection. Then create Monday's domino and attach it to the Daily Domino display for the day. Allow for an extended discussion once a week.

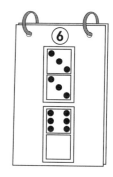

UPDATE PROCEDURE

Each day of the month attach a new Blank Domino Card (TR5) on the ones side of the Daily Domino. Encourage volunteers to suggest an arrangement of dots to place on each half of the Blank Domino to create a total equal to the date—for example, a total of one dot on the first, two dots on the second, three dots on the third, and so on. On the 10th, move the domino showing a sum of ten dots to the tens side and attach a Blank Domino on the ones side. On the 11th, create on the ones side a domino with just one dot. Continue to create a domino each day, showing a new combination whenever possible and moving a ten domino to the tens place on the 20th and the 30th.

Each day remove yesterday's domino and attach it to one of the 9" × 12" display papers for the sums 1 through 10. During the second ten days of the month, the class will refer to the sheets to make sure each day's domino shows a different combination for the day's sum. The domino for one will have to be repeated (since we consider 1 + 0 to be the same as 0 + 1), but a second way can be found to form dominoes for two or more dots. During the last ten days of the month, no new ways will be found for one, two, or three, but new combinations can still be found for sums greater than three.

DISCUSSION EARLY IN THE MONTH

Tell children that they will be investigating how many different ways they can make dominoes with one to ten dots. To get the class started thinking about the possibilities for combinations to come, display the sheets showing the dominoes completed during the first few days and ask:

▶   Are there any other ways we can make a one-dot domino, if we agree that a 1 + 0 domino is the same as a 0 + 1 domino?

▶   What about three dots? What will all the three-dot dominoes look like?

▶   How many four-dot dominoes do you think we will be able to make? What makes you think so?

DISCUSSION DURING THE MONTH

To help children focus on the combination for the day, cover half of the domino and tell a subtraction story. For example, on the 26th you might say, "I have six pennies. You see five. How many are missing?" or, "I need six buttons. I have five. How many more do I need?" To reinforce more ways to make six, tell similar stories to go with the dominoes attached to the "6" display paper.

DISCUSSION FOR THE END OF THE MONTH

Display all the sheets of dominoes for sums one through ten. Beginning with one, ask the class to decide if they made all the possible dominoes for each number. Starting with six, there will be at least one possible combination missing. To encourage thinking, you might initiate a discussion similar to the one that follows:

SAMPLE DISCUSSION

Teacher: Let's look at six. Do we have all the dominoes we can possibly put together for six? Which ones do we have?

Child: We have a five and one.

Child: We have a three and three.

Child: And we have a six and zero.

Teacher: Can anyone think of another combination we can make for six?

Child: We don't have a four and two.

Teacher: No, we don't. If we were to make a two and four domino the next time we make a domino for six, then would we have all the possible dominoes for six? Would we have dominoes showing 6, 5, 4, 3, 2, 1, and 0 as part of six?

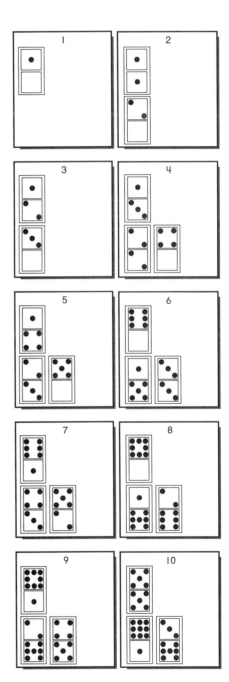

At other times do the same for seven through ten. Suggest that children look for a pattern that would help them to be sure that all the possible combinations for each number have been found. Remind them that they'll have a chance to propose some of these unused combinations for the Daily Domino in May.

HELPFUL HINTS

▶ Some teachers use multiple copies of TR5 and TR6 to let children create their own domino books. The books include a page for each sum to ten. Each day's domino can be pasted on the appropriate page until all the combinations for sums one to ten are represented by domino pictures. Over the summer, parents and children can play number guessing games using the book—for example, "I'm thinking of a domino on the nine page that has four dots on one half. What's on the domino?" or "I'm looking at the five page. How many dominoes do I see?"

▶ *What's Left in the Can?* This activity provides experience in figuring out the missing part of a total by counting on when children know one part. Using a number equal to the total on the day's domino, a volunteer drops pennies into a can as children count the "klink, klink . . ." Another child then takes some pennies out and shows them to the class. Everyone tries to determine how many are left in the can. Following a "thinking time," children whisper their prediction to a neighbor. Then everyone counts on, keeping track on their fingers to confirm the amount left in the can. For example, on the seventh, with three pennies in view, the class counts, "4, 5, 6, 7; 4 are in the can." A volunteer empties the can to prove it.

▶ Children can use Domino Halves (TR6) pasted to Domino Blanks (TR5) to create Fact Flash Cards showing all the addition combinations for each sum to 10. Children should write the addition fact without the sum on the back of each card. They can organize their cards in envelopes and keep them handy for frequent practice.

▶ A wide variety of hands-on activities that acquaint children with combinations to ten and develop what Robert Wirtz often referred to as "friendliness with numbers" can be found in the following resources, classics in the field: *Developing Number Concepts Using Unifix Cubes,* by Kathy Richardson, Addison-Wesley, 1984; *Drill and Practice at a Problem-Solving Level;* by Robert Wirtz, Curriculum Development Associates, 1975; *Mathematics Their Way,* Chapters 7–9, by Mary Baratta-Lorton, Addison-Wesley, 1976.

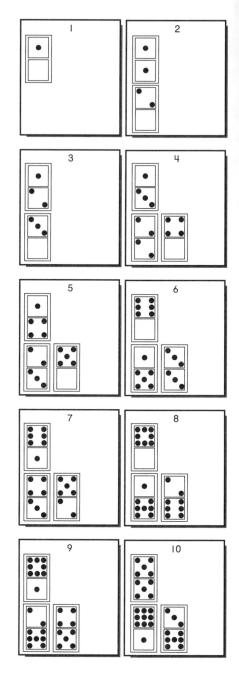

Today, the length of our tape measure is __7__ inches, the same as a _pencil._

FOCUS

▶ Estimating and measuring length in nonstandard and standard units (inches)
▶ Comparing the lengths of common objects
▶ Matching 12 inches with a foot ruler

MATERIALS

Three 3" × 10" strips of Inch Squared Paper (TR11) attached to form a 30-inch strip, watercolor pens in two colors, masking tape or fun tack, common objects of varying lengths.

OVERVIEW

In this element, children will have the chance to help construct a measuring tape that increases in length one inch every day of the month.

FREQUENCY

Update daily. On Mondays, add 3 inches to the tape for Saturday, Sunday, and Monday. Discuss daily until the 12th of the month and twice a week in later weeks.

UPDATE PROCEDURE

Each day color in one square inch along the center row of the blank 3" × 30" grid, which can be attached above the chalk tray or below a windowsill or counter edge. Alternate colors every five squares to make it easier to read from a distance. Record the day's measurement near the tape. "Today the length of our tape measure is _____ inches."

DISCUSSION EARLY IN THE MONTH

As often as possible, follow the Update Procedure with an estimation activity. Have children (from their seats) look around the room for objects that might match the colored inches on the tape for the day. Allow two or three children to bring up objects they have found (those that can be moved). Before each object is matched to the tape, ask the class to predict if it will be too long, too short, or just right (within a half inch). If an object's length matches the day's tape to the nearest inch, it remains next to the tape for all to see throughout the day. If none of the objects are close enough, do not place anything by the tape at this time. Perhaps something will be found during a later activity period.

DISCUSSION FOR THE TWELFTH OF APRIL

If no one suggests a ruler to match the tape's length on this day, bring one out and place it on the tape so children can see that the ruler is exactly 12 inches long. You might devote all the time on this day to measuring. Pass out rulers, and let children measure the length of their own feet to compare to the standard "foot" ruler. They may need to be reminded to line up their heel with the "zero" end of the ruler.

DISCUSSION LATER IN THE MONTH

As the length of the tape increases, finding objects to match becomes difficult. When this happens, stop searching for objects of a specific length. Instead, have the class guess and check the length of a common object drawn from a collection box of items (paintbrush, ribbon, scissors, etc.) placed near the tape. After estimates have been made, a volunteer can model how to match one end of the object exactly with the end of the tape and read the tape to the nearest inch.

HELPFUL HINTS

▶ On the 12th, some teachers glue a ruler to a 12-inch cardboard foot cutout that can rest on the measuring tape throughout the day. This helps everyone remember that the 12-inch ruler is equal to one "foot."

▶ Sometimes children suggest objects that cannot be brought to the tape (a drawer handle, height of paper towel holder, etc.). They can cut string equal to the length of the object they cannot pick up and bring the string to the tape to confirm their measure. String also works well for estimating and checking the length of curves and circumferences.

▶ Linda Anderson, a teacher in New Orleans, has her students keep their own records, coloring in one inch each day on their individual one-foot tapes (made from TR11). Children use their tapes to look for things in the room equal to the day's measure. Linda creates a list of each day's findings and hangs it from a clothesline in her room.

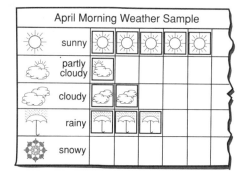

EVERY DAY ELEMENT

GRAPH

FOCUS

▶ Collecting and recording data on a graph over time
▶ Reading and interpreting data on a picture or bar graph
▶ Counting and comparing small quantities

MATERIALS

Every Day Graph (TR9) made to match the ones assembled in October and January for sampling the weather, Weather Markers (TR12)

OVERVIEW

The Every Day Graph provides a record of a weather sample in October, January, and April. Graphing the weather again this month allows the class the opportunity to compare the kinds of weather that occurred in your area in the fall and winter with the kinds of weather that appear in the spring.

FREQUENCY

Update daily and discuss once a week.

UPDATE PROCEDURE

Once again have the class look outside at the same time each day and decide what the weather is like at that moment. Have a volunteer attach the appropriate Weather Marker to the Graph.

DISCUSSION FOR THE FIRST DAY

Instead of preparing the Weather Graph ahead of time, involve children in setting it up. Tell children you want to create a graph that has the same headings in the same order as the October and January Weather Graphs so that it will be easy to compare the information gathered during the three different seasons. With the old graphs in view, allow the children to tell you how to label the new April Graph. Ask if they think the same length will work out or if they think it will need to be longer or shorter and why. Place the first day's Weather Marker on the Graph.

Looking at the October and January Graphs, ask the class to indicate by a show of hands who thinks there will be more sunny days in the April sample than in the fall and winter samples. How about rainy days—more, fewer, or the same? How about snowy days? And so on. It will be interesting to see how the three weather samples compare by month's end.

DISCUSSION DURING THE MONTH

Refer to October's Discussion (page 21).

DISCUSSION FOR THE END OF THE MONTH

Focus student attention on the three graphs showing fall, winter, and spring weather samples. Before making any comparisons, count up the total days represented on each graph to make sure the samples are close enough in size to allow fair comparisons. (Each graph should have 17 to 20 Weather Markers.) You might start with an open-ended question such as, "What do we know about our fall, winter, and spring weather from the samples shown on these graphs? What do these graphs tell us?" After children have offered many observations and comparisons of their own, you might follow up with a few questions:

▶ Which month had the most sunny days?
▶ Which month had nearly the same number of partly cloudy and sunny days?
▶ Which month had the most rainy days? The fewest?
▶ Which months have the same total of cloudy and rainy days together?
▶ Which were the best months for riding a bike?
▶ Which month had the most of your favorite weather?

HELPFUL HINTS

▶ If your school year includes a vacation break in April, you'll need to keep a record of the weather during vacation. Otherwise, the April sample at month's end will be too small to compare to the October and January data.
▶ As suggested in January, you may want to use the newspaper to graph the weather of a city in another part of the country to compare to your own spring weather. (See January, page 53.)

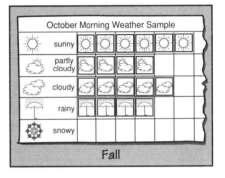

Fall

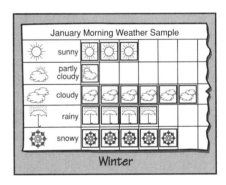

Winter

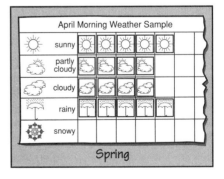

Spring

FINISHING UP

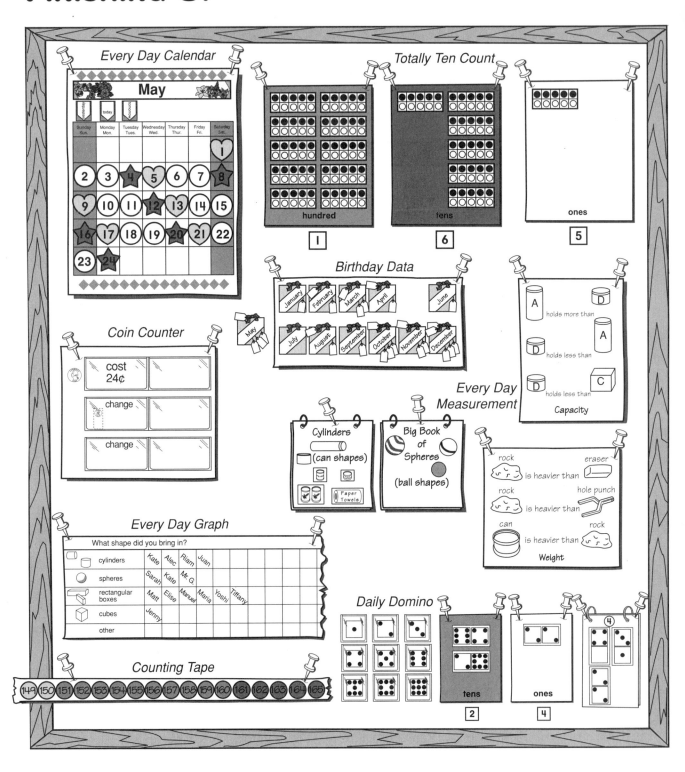

This month's measurement activities focus on comparing and measuring capacity and weight. The Coin Counter provides a new experience in figuring change for purchases. The Graph provides motivation for the class to search for geometric shapes. Graphing everyone's responses to the question, "Which part of Calendar Math helped me learn the most?" might provide a fitting end-of-the-year activity. While no two groups are alike, children's answers might help you to evaluate your successes and to plan modifications for next year.

EVERY DAY ELEMENT

COUNTING TAPE

152 153 154 155 156 157 158 159 160 161 162 163 164 165

FOCUS

▶ Developing number sense
▶ Counting with one-to-one correspondence
▶ Grouping and counting by 10's and 1's
▶ Understanding place value
▶ Comparing and ordering quantities
▶ Counting on and counting back
▶ Extending number patterns and using mental math
▶ Solving problems

The MATERIALS, FREQUENCY, and UPDATE PROCEDURE for the Counting Tape continue from September. See September, pages 2 and 3.

DISCUSSION DURING THE MONTH

Continue to focus on ways the counting pattern for numbers above 100 is like the sequence for numbers up to 100. See March, page 70 for discussion suggestions.

HELPFUL HINTS

▶ On one of the last days of school, focus the activity on taking down the Counting Tape. Begin to cut the Tape in 10-number intervals, handing out strips (1–10, 11–20, 21–30, and so on) to individual children. Some teachers have the class help construct a giant hundred chart. Children pin up the decade strips of Counting Tape in order, one below the other, ending with 91–100. If holes are punched near the ends of the strips, the strips can be slipped off pins for ordering activities and can then be easily returned to the display. The giant hundred chart provides a focus for pattern searches, which help children see the predictability of the counting sequence.

▶ Children can color their own Hundred Chart (TR16) to match the large one formed with the cut-apart Counting Tape. The children's copies can accompany them home in June and be used to mark off the days of summer vacation. Children can consider the question, "Do you think we will have marked off 100 days away from school before we come back again at the end of summer?"

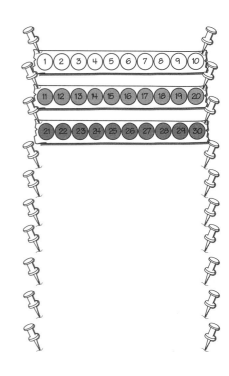

EVERY DAY ELEMENT

TOTALLY TEN COUNT

FOCUS
▶ Developing number sense
▶ Grouping and counting by 10's, 5's, and 1's
▶ Understanding place value
▶ Learning addition combinations for sums 5 through 10
▶ Adding or subtracting 10 and 100 using place value models
▶ Using mental math

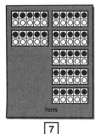

The MATERIALS, FREQUENCY, UPDATE PROCEDURE, and DISCUSSIONS DURING THE MONTH continue for the Totally Ten Count from past months. See October, pages 14 and 15, November, page 25, and March, page 71, for possible questioning strategies.

HELPFUL HINT
▶ If you need display space for the Daily Domino and the large hundred chart (see Counting Tape, page 93), you might consider retiring the Totally Ten Count for the rest of the year. Its main goal has been met.

EVERY DAY ELEMENT

CALENDAR

FOCUS
▶ Recognizing, analyzing, and predicting patterns
▶ Knowing the days of the week in order
▶ Counting with one-to-one correspondence
▶ Counting on and counting back
▶ Matching quantities with numerals
▶ Solving problems

MATERIALS
Every Day Calendar, May and June Month Strips, May and June Calendar Pieces; or heart, circle, star, hexagon, and square shapes from Calendar Cutouts (TR21); Today, Yesterday, and Tomorrow Markers (TR21), Calendar Record (TR15)

SUGGESTED PATTERN FOR MAY
The May Calendar Pieces use red hearts, white circles, and blue stars to create an ABBC pattern in the order red heart, white circle, white circle, blue star.

SUGGESTED PATTERN FOR JUNE
The June Calendar Pieces use yellow hexagons, blue stars, and orange squares to create an AABBC pattern in the order yellow hexagon, yellow hexagon, blue star, blue star, orange square.

If you choose to use the shapes from the Calendar Cutouts (TR21) in May and June, you can use the same or any other set of five colors to create the patterns. Write the dates on the pieces before posting.

The FREQUENCY and UPDATE PROCEDURE for the Calendar continue from November. See page 26 for a detailed description.

DISCUSSION FOR THE END OF THE SECOND WEEK OF MAY

Explain that a new pattern appears on the May Calendar. In addition to asking children to predict the next day's piece, ask them to determine the color and shape of the piece that will appear in one week, two weeks, or on the last day of the month. This encourages a variety of counting on and mental math strategies. Invite children to share how they came up with their predictions.

Continue to encourage children to suggest and try different ideas for acting out the pattern, assigning different body motions to the A, B, and C. (See September, page 8.) At other times, have children use various art materials, collections, or other manipulatives to create a version of the month's ABBC pattern on their own.

DISCUSSION FOR THE END OF MAY

On one of the last days of May, ask children to look for some patterns on the Calendar. The color pattern will make several diagonals stand out. The multiples of 4 will all be the same color and shape. Each diagonal will show a pattern increasing by 8 from one number to the next.

DISCUSSION FOR THE BEGINNING OF JUNE

Any time after the fifth of June, when the pattern has started to repeat, the Calendar can be used to encourage more problem solving. Each day, as a new shape goes up, ask children to predict the number and shape that will come up in one week, two weeks, and three weeks. After entertaining suggestions, place the shapes for these future days on the Calendar. Allow time for children to explain how they were able to predict the number and the shape.

HELPFUL HINTS

▶ The Calendar Pieces can be used to interest children in exploring spatial relationships. To get children looking for symmetry in two-dimensional shapes, begin with the Heart Calendar Piece. Demonstrate how folding it down the center can be a test for symmetry. If the two halves are congruent, matching up exactly, the fold is a line of symmetry. Let them experiment with the circle, star, square, and hexagon pieces to see if they can fold them into matching congruent halves and find some of their lines of symmetry.

Hearts have stars under them.
The circles come in 2's. When you see one, you know the next one will be a circle, too.
The stars go by 4's: 4, 8, 12, 16, 20, . . .
The pattern goes heart, circle, circle, star.
The hearts go down 9, 17, 25, and 5, 13, 21.
The hearts go 1, 5, 9, 13, 17 . .plus 4's.

EVERY DAY ELEMENT   BIRTHDAY DATA

FOCUS

▶ Knowing the months of the year in order
▶ Counting with one-to-one correpondence to 31
▶ Reading, comparing, and ordering numbers to 31
▶ Solving problems and using mental math
▶ Interpreting organized data

The MATERIALS and FREQUENCY for the Birthday Data continue from September and October. (See page 9 and page 18.)

UPDATE PROCEDURE
At the beginning of May, have the class point out the Birthday Package that matches the month written above the Calendar. Have the class name the months in order, beginning with January. Go through the sequence again, stopping with a clap on the present month. Note that May is the fifth month of the year.

After practicing the sequence of all the months, take May's Package out of the array and feature it near the Calendar. Children then predict where the birthdays will appear on the Calendar, explain how they came up with their predictions, and mark the birthdays with the tags taken from the May Package.

DISCUSSION FOR THE BEGINNING OF THE MONTH
See September, page 10, for discussion questions to accompany the identification of the month's birthdays on the Calendar.

DISCUSSION DURING THE MONTH
Continue to use the Packages as a focus for problem solving. Ask questions that involve children in adding and comparing the numbers of tags on the different Birthday Packages. Occasionally encourage volunteers to pose the questions. (See March, page 73 and April, page 84.)

HELPFUL HINT
► If your school year extends into June, use the Update Procedure at the beginning of the month. Mention that June signals an end to spring and the beginning of summer.

EVERY DAY ELEMENT

COIN COUNTER

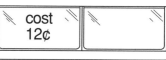

FOCUS
► Knowing the penny, nickel, dime, and quarter
► Knowing the value of each coin and coin equivalencies
► Counting by 10's, 5's, and 1's
► Adding mixed coins
► Using mental math, including figuring change
► Recording money amounts using both the dollar sign and decimal point and the cent sign
► Solving problems using coins

The MATERIALS and FREQUENCY for the Coin Counter continue from March. See page 74 for a detailed description.

OVERVIEW
This month the focus is figuring change when a purchase is made with a quarter—now that children have had sufficient practice creating combinations of coins equal to the day's date in March and April. Counting change fosters counting up and other mental math strategies.

UPDATE PROCEDURE

Through May 25, the top row of the Coin Counter displays the cost of an imaginary purchase equal to the day's date in cents. Tell children that this is the amount the clerk keeps when a quarter is used to pay for the purchase. The task each day is for children to determine the correct change due by counting on from the amount of purchase to 25. For example, on May 12, the top row displays a 12¢ purchase. To show making change from a quarter, place 3 pennies into the second row of the Counter as the class counts up, "13, 14, 15," and then 2 nickels, perhaps, as the class continues, "20, 25 cents." Children can suggest other possible combinations of coins that the clerk could use to count out the correct change. One of these alternatives can be displayed in the remaining pocket of the Coin Counter and counted up.

HELPFUL HINT

▶ The play store is a great opportunity for children to use calculators to confirm the amount of their purchases and their change.

EVERY DAY ELEMENT

DAILY DOMINO

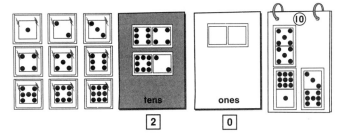

FOCUS

▶ Seeing part and whole relationships
▶ Working with addition combinations to 10
▶ Solving problems

The MATERIALS, FREQUENCY, and UPDATE PROCEDURE for the Daily Domino continue from April. See April, page 86.

DISCUSSION FOR THE BEGINNING OF THE MONTH

Tell children they will continue to investigate how many different ways they can make dominoes with 1–10 dots. To get the class started thinking about the possibilities for combinations to come, display the sheets showing the dominoes completed in April for the numbers 1–6 and ask questions similar to the following:

▶ Are there any other ways we can make a one-dot domino? (Remember, we agree that a 1 + 0 domino is the same as a 0 + 1 domino.)
▶ What do all the three-dot dominoes look like? Do we have all the dominoes showing 3, 2, 1, and 0 on one side?
▶ Did we make all the possible combinations? Did we make all the dominoes showing 4, 3, 2, 1, and 0 on one side?
▶ What day will it be when we can suggest a new domino?

DISCUSSION DURING THE MONTH

On the days when a domino not seen before is proposed and constructed, have children share how they knew there was still a missing combination and how they came up with the number of dots to put on each side. (There are still more combinations to be found this month for the sums 6–10, so May 6th through the 10th and May 18th through the 20th will be the days to discover them.) After the 20th, all the possible dominoes for the sums to ten will have been completed, so any domino combination that displays the correct amount on the ones side of the Daily Domino can be used.

DISCUSSION FOR THE END OF THE MONTH

Display all the sheets of dominoes for sums one through ten.
Beginning with one, ask the class to decide if all the possible
dominoes have been made for the numbers one through ten.
Consider giving each child a Blank Domino and some counters.
It's a lot easier to be sure you have found all the ways to make six,
for example, if you can start with six real objects on one side and
then move one of them over at a time changing 6 + 0 to 5 + 1, to 4
+ 2, to 3 + 3, to 2 + 4, to 1 + 5, to 0 + 6. Keeping in mind that the
"turnarounds" (such as 5 + 1 and 1 + 5) only need to be represented once, children can check to see if all the combinations they find
with the counters are shown on the display dominoes.

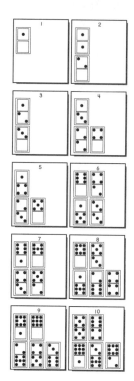

HELPFUL HINTS

▶ Play *Guess My Domino*, similar to *What's Left in the Can?* (see
April, page 88). This activity encourages counting on and
develops familiarity with addition combinations. Give the
children clues such as the following:

   ▶   I have 3 dots and 6 dots. What's my sum?

▶ If children are adding the day's new domino to their own
Domino Books (April Helpful Hints, page 88), allow time for
them to update their books on May 6th through the 10th and
May 18th through the 20th.

EVERY DAY ELEMENT   MEASUREMENT

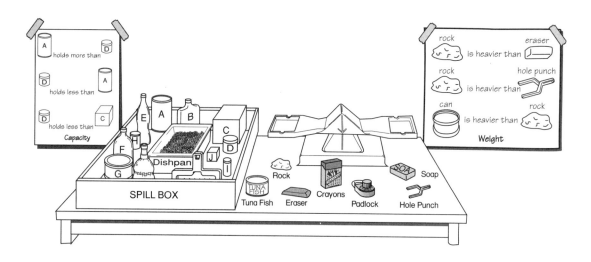

FOCUS

▶ Estimating and comparing capacity and weight

MATERIALS

A container of rice placed in a large shallow box; a funnel, dust-
pan, and whisk broom; a collection of containers of different
shapes and sizes labeled *A, B, C,* etc.; a balance scale; a collection
of common objects in different shapes, sizes, and weights labeled
A, B, C, etc. (for example, can of tuna, box of crayons, hole punch,
chalkboard eraser, etc.); two 17" × 11" record sheets.

OVERVIEW

This month children explore capacity and weight, comparing the capacities of different containers and the weights of different objects on alternate days. Everyone has a chance to predict which of two containers holds more or which of two objects weighs more and then watch the comparisons be made.

FREQUENCY

Each day the class predicts and compares either capacity or weight. Discuss each time.

UPDATE PROCEDURE

Invite a volunteer to assist with the measuring.

Capacity: Show the class one container that you have filled with rice and a second empty container of a different shape. Ask the class to predict what will happen when the full container is emptied into the empty one.

Record the number of guesses for each on the chalkboard. Let the volunteer do the pouring. Record the results.

Weight: Show the class two objects varying in size and weight. Have the class guess which object is heavier. Record the number of guesses for each object. Let the volunteer place the objects on each side of the balance scale so children can check their predictions. Record the results.

DISCUSSION THROUGHOUT THE MONTH

Capacity: Talk about the results of comparing the two containers. Here are some questions you might ask the children:

▶ Was anyone surprised at the results? How so?
▶ Did the height or "tallness" of the container matter to you when you made your guess?
▶ Did you pay more attention to how "fat" or wide the container was when you made your guess?
▶ Do you think a taller container will always hold more than a shorter one?
▶ Did anyone use comparisons made on days earlier in the month to help with today's guess? What helped you?

Finally, look at the record of the guesses to see if the day's prediction was easy or difficult to make.

Weight: Talk about the day's results. Ask children to share why they guessed as they did. Sample questions follow:

▶ Did the size of the object influence your guess?
▶ Will the larger of two objects always be the heavier?
▶ Did anyone think about having held similar objects before and how heavy they felt in your hands?
▶ Did anyone use past days' comparisons to help make a guess today?

DISCUSSION FOR THE END OF THE MONTH

Capacity: At month's end, have the class guess which container holds the most. Let a volunteer take the chosen container and compare it with each of the others. If a different container is found to hold more, use it to compare with the remaining containers.

Weight: Ask children to think about all the objects that have been paired up on the scale and to guess which one weighs the most. Let volunteers take the object that receives the greatest number of guesses and compare its weight to the weights of the other objects using the scale. If a heavier object is found, use it to make comparisons with the remaining objects. At other times, allow children to lift the objects and use the scales to make comparisons.

HELPFUL HINT

▶ Include the use of nonstandard units by having children tally the number of scoops required to fill the jars. Use the results to make comparisons and order the jars by their capacities. To the weighing setup add a container of ceramic tile, large metal washers, or wooden cubes, which can serve as nonstandard units of weight. Children can place an object on one side of the scale and the nonstandard units on the other side until both sides balance. Then units can be removed, grouped into tens, and counted. The results can be used to compare and order the objects by their weights.

EVERY DAY ELEMENT

FOCUS

▶ Recognizing three-dimensional and two-dimensional geometric shapes in the environment
▶ Describing attributes of cylinders, spheres, rectangular solids, and cubes
▶ Identifying and naming circles, rectangles, and squares

MATERIALS

A collection of boxes, containers, and objects that are cylinders, spheres, rectangular solids, or cubes; Every Day Graph (TR9); class set of graph markers ($1\frac{3}{4}$" paper squares); watercolor pen; four large posters, one for each shape; advertising supplements from a Sunday newspaper; models of geometric solids (optional)

OVERVIEW

This month children are introduced to cylinders, spheres, rectangular solids, and cubes. Each child will have the chance to bring one object from home that fits into one of the categories of shapes. The growth of the class collection of shapes will be recorded on a graph. The emphasis throughout the month will be on modeling and eliciting descriptive geometric language used to distinguish one set of shapes from another.

FREQUENCY

After the Parent Letter goes home (see Helpful Hints), update daily and discuss as often as time allows.

GRAPH

What shape did you bring in?				
cylinders	Kate	Alec	Riam	
spheres	Sarah	Kate	Mr. G.	
rectangular boxes	Matt	Elise		
cubes	Jenny			
other				

UPDATE PROCEDURE

After the shapes have been introduced and the Parent Letter sent home, ask each day for the children who have brought items to come forward with their objects. Have the group classify each object as a can-shaped cylinder, a ball-shaped sphere, a box-shaped rectangular solid, a square-box-shaped cube, or "other." Let children justify their classifications. Finally, have the day's contributors add markers to the Every Day Graph to represent each shape brought in that day. Ask the class to suggest a few facts revealed by the Graph.

DISCUSSION FOR THE BEGINNING OF THE MONTH

Explain that this month the class will be searching for four different geometric shapes at school and at home. Introduce one shape each day. Show the class two or three examples of one of the shapes and have children tell how they are alike. Add your observations, if needed, so the critical attributes of each shape will be pointed out:

For cylinders (cans, spice jars, batteries, coins, etc.):
- ▶ They're round and they roll.
- ▶ The faces or openings on the two ends are matching circles.
- ▶ They'll stand on their circle faces.

For spheres (globe, playground ball, orange, marble, etc.):
- ▶ They're round and they roll.
- ▶ They have no flat faces and will not stack.
- ▶ Each has one continuous curved surface.

For rectangular solids (school box, brick, chalkboard eraser, etc.):
- ▶ They have six flat faces.
- ▶ The faces are in the shape of rectangles (four sides with four square corners).
- ▶ They stack easily and do not roll.

For cubes (sugar cube, cubic boxes, wooden cube, etc.):
- ▶ They are all rectangular solids.
- ▶ Their faces are all special rectangles called squares (four equal sides and four square corners).

Follow this discussion of the attributes with a search for other examples of the three-dimensional shape in the classroom.

When all four shapes have been introduced, label a poster with the name and sketch of each shape. Invite children to cut out pictures of common objects that represent cylinders, spheres, boxes, and cubes from newspaper advertising supplements. Paste these pictures of real-world geometric solids on the appropriate poster.

DISCUSSION THROUGHOUT THE MONTH

Have children look for a discarded item at home that can be added to the class collection of cylinders, spheres, rectangular solids, and cubes. The object must be something that doesn't need to be returned. (See the sample letter to parents on page 102.) Assemble an Every Day Graph and label the rows with the names of the shapes to record the contributions as they come in.

When children begin to bring in their objects from home, follow up the Update Procedure, in which the objects are classified, with a discussion of the emerging graph whenever possible. Some questions might include:

▶ How many items have been brought in so far? How did you get your total or sum?
▶ What shape do we have the most of now?
▶ What shape do we have the least of in our class collection?
▶ How many more _____ than _____ do we have?
▶ If you could use the class collection of shapes, what would you want to build with them?

HELPFUL HINTS

▶ The following note to parents is a sample that can be adapted to fit your needs.

Dear Parents,
   We've been learning to recognize and describe the following geometric shapes in class this month:

— Cylinders
   (can shapes)
— Spheres
   (ball shapes)
— Rectangular solids
   (box shapes)
— Cubes
   (square box shapes)

Please encourage your child to point out objects in your home that can be classified as cylinders, spheres, rectangular boxes, cubes. The children have been asked to look for a discarded household item headed for the garbage or recycling bin and bring it in to add to the class collection of real-world boxes, cylinders, and spheres.

   Thanks for your support with this project. Please do not send anything made of glass.

                    Sincerely,

▶ Children enjoy problem solving in the game *Who Am I?* Ask everyone to look at the class collection of objects. Give them clues, which, when taken together, identify one and only one object. For example, "I am a rectangular solid, larger than the raisin box, and I used to hold a breakfast food," might narrow the selection to the cereal box.

Assessment Alternatives in Mathematics: An overview of assessment techniques that promote learning. Berkeley, CA: Regents, University of California, 1989.

Baratta-Lorton, Mary. "The Opening," *Math Their Way Newsletter 1977–78.* Saratoga, CA: The Center for Innovation in Education.

Baratta-Lorton, Mary. *Workjobs II and Mathematics Their Way.* Reading, MA: Addison-Wesley, 1978, 1976.

Burk, Donna, Allyn Snider, and Paula Symonds. "The Calendar," *Box It or Bag It.* Salem, OR: Math Learning Center, 1988.

Burns, Marilyn. *The Math Solution.* Sausalito, CA: Marilyn Burns and Associates, 1981.

Burns, Marilyn, and Kathy Richardson. "Making Sense out of Word Problems," *Learning.* January, 1981.

Curriculum Development Associates, Inc. *Making Friends with Numbers,* Washington, DC: Curriculum Development Associated, Inc., 1979.

For Good Measure: Principles and Goals for Mathematics Assessment. Washington, DC: National Academy Press.

Kamii, Constance. *Young Children Reinvent Arithmetic: Implications of Piaget's Theory.* New York: Teachers College Press, 1985.

Kanter, Patsy. *Helping Your Child Learn Math.* U.S. Department of Education, 1992.

Marolda, Maria. *Attribute Games and Activities.* Mountain View, CA: Creative Pub., 1976.

Mathematical Sciences Education Board, National Research Council. *Measuring Up: Prototypes for Mathematics Assessments.* Washington, DC: National Academy Press, 1993.

National Council of Teachers of Mathematics. *Assessment in the Mathematics Classroom, The 1993 Yearbook.* Reston, VA: The National Council of Teachers of Mathematics, 1993.

National Council of Teachers of Mathematics. *Curriculum and Evaluation Standards for School Mathematics.* Reston, VA: The National Council of Teachers of Mathematics, 1989.

National Council of Teachers of Mathematics. *Mathematics Assessment: Myths, Models, Good Questions and Practical Suggestions.* Reston, VA: The National Council of Teachers of Mathematics, 1991.

The National Council of Teachers of Mathematics. *Professional Standards for Teaching Mathematics.* Reston, VA: The National Council of Teachers of Mathematics, 1991.

Richardson, Kathy. *A Look at Children's Thinking. Video 2 Assessment Techniques: Number Combinations and Place Value.* Norman, OK: Educational Enrichment, Inc. 1990.

Richardson, Kathy. *Developing Number Concepts Using Unifix Cubes.* Reading, MA: Addison-Wesley, 1984.

Stevenson, Robert Louis. *Block City.* New York: Dutton Children's Books, 1988.

Wirtz, Robert. *Banking on Problem Solving and Think, Talk, Connect.* Washington, DC: Curriculum Development Assoc., Inc., 1980.

Wirtz, Robert. *Drill and Practice at a Problem-Solving Level.* Washington, DC: Curriculum Development Assoc., Inc., 1976.

Wirtz, Robert. *Making Friends with Numbers, Kit 1: Addition and Subtraction.* Washington, DC: Curriculum Development Assoc., Inc. 1977.

TR1 Birthday Package and Gift Tags
TR2 Date Cards
TR3 Coin Cards
TR4 0–9 Digit Cards/Numeral Dot Cards
TR5 Domino Blanks
TR6 Domino Halves
TR7 Totally Ten Grids
TR8 Every Day Clock
TR9 Every Day Graph
TR10 A.M./P.M. Chart
TR11 Inch Squared Paper
TR12 Weather/Shoe Markers
TR13 Bank/Purse Backgrounds
TR14 Jar/Box Backgrounds
TR15 Calendar Record
TR16 Hundred Chart
TR17 Demo Coins: Quarter and Dime, Heads
TR18 Demo Coins: Quarter and Dime, Tails
TR19 Demo Coins: Nickel and Penny, Heads
TR20 Demo Coins: Nickel and Penny, Tails
TR21 Calendar Cutouts
TR22 Calendar Cutouts
TR23 Blank Hundred Chart
TR24 Coin Comparing Cards
TR25 Ten Grid Number Cards
TR26 Centimeter Squared Paper
TR27 Pattern Block Rhombuses/Triangles
TR28 Pattern Block Hexagons/Trapezoids
TR29 Geodot Paper
TR30 Mini Clock Records
TR31 Post Office Materials

DAYS OF THE WEEK IN SPANISH

Sunday	domingo
Monday	lunes
Tuesday	martes
Wednesday	miércoles
Thursday	jueves
Friday	viernes
Saturday	sábado

NUMBERS THROUGH 31 IN SPANISH

zero	cero
one	uno
two	dos
three	tres
four	cuatro
five	cinco
six	seis
seven	siete
eight	ocho
nine	nueve
ten	diez
eleven	once
twelve	doce
thirteen	trece
fourteen	catorce
fifteen	quince
sixteen	diez y seis
seventeen	diez y siete
eighteen	diez y ocho
nineteen	diez y nueve
twenty	viente
twenty-one	viente y uno
twenty-two	viente y dos
twenty-three	viente y tres
twenty-four	viente y cuatro
twenty-five	viente y cinco
twenty-six	viente y seis
twenty-seven	viente y siete
twenty-eight	viente y ocho
twenty-nine	viente y nueve
thirty	treinta
thirty-one	treinta y uno

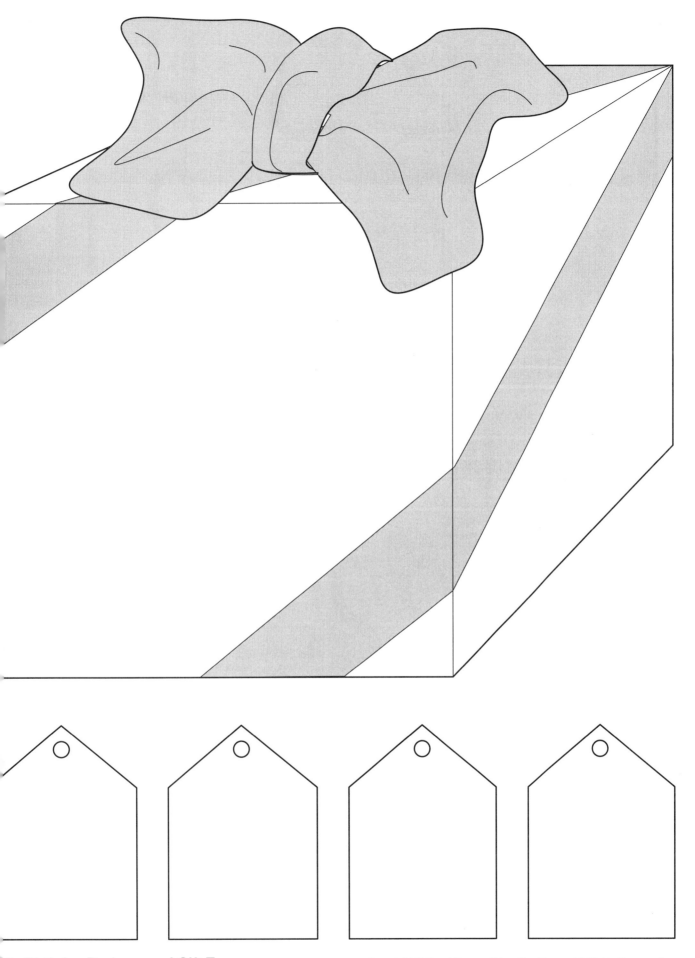

Copyright © Great Source Education Group. All Rights Reserved.

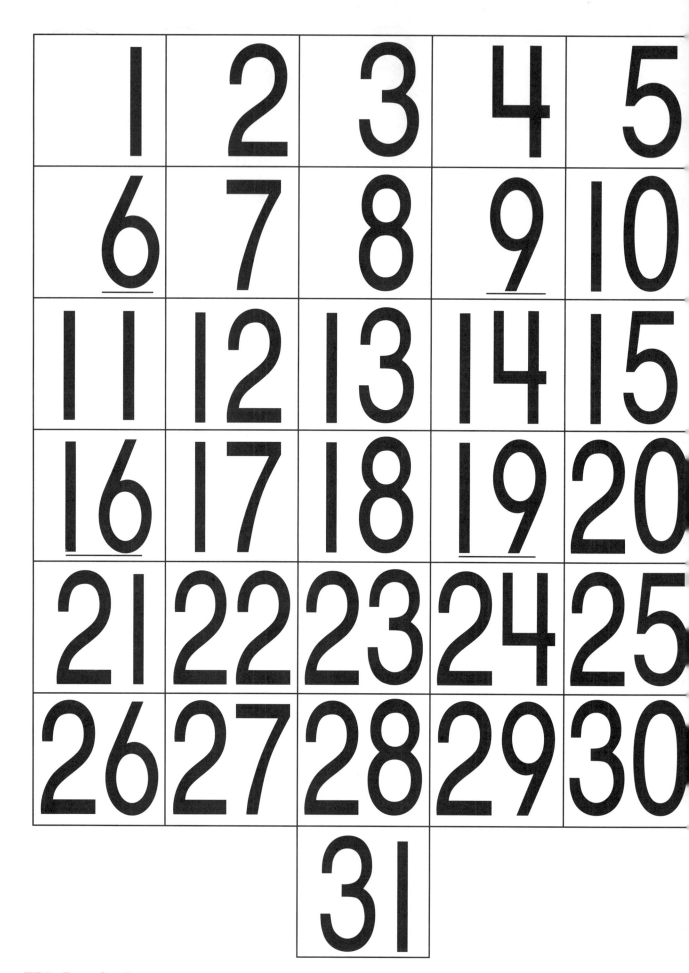

Copyright © Great Source Education Group. All Rights Reserved

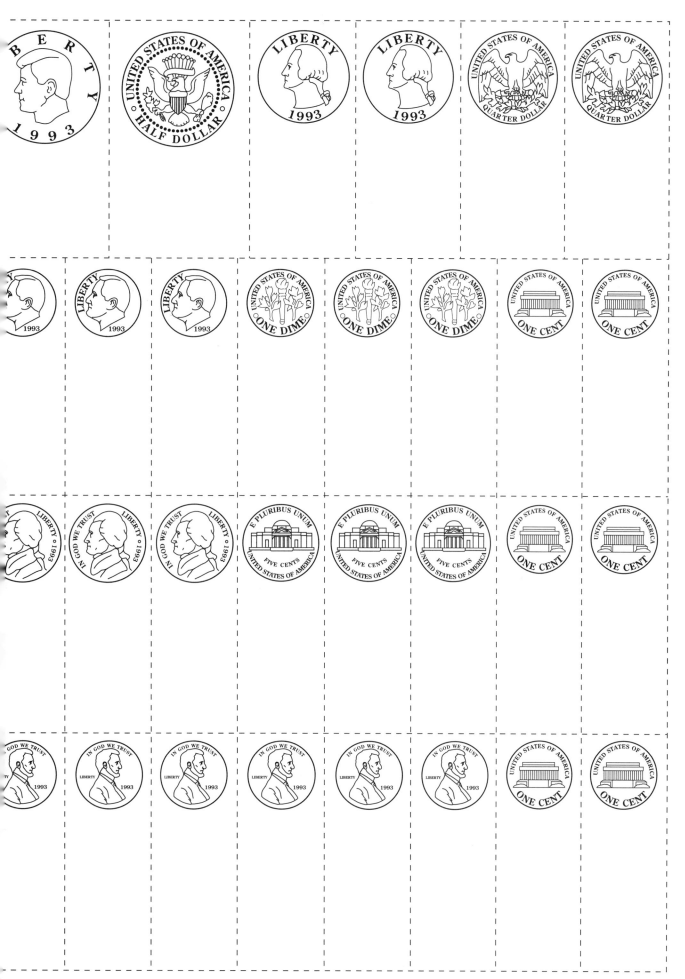

Copyright © Great Source Education Group. All Rights Reserved.

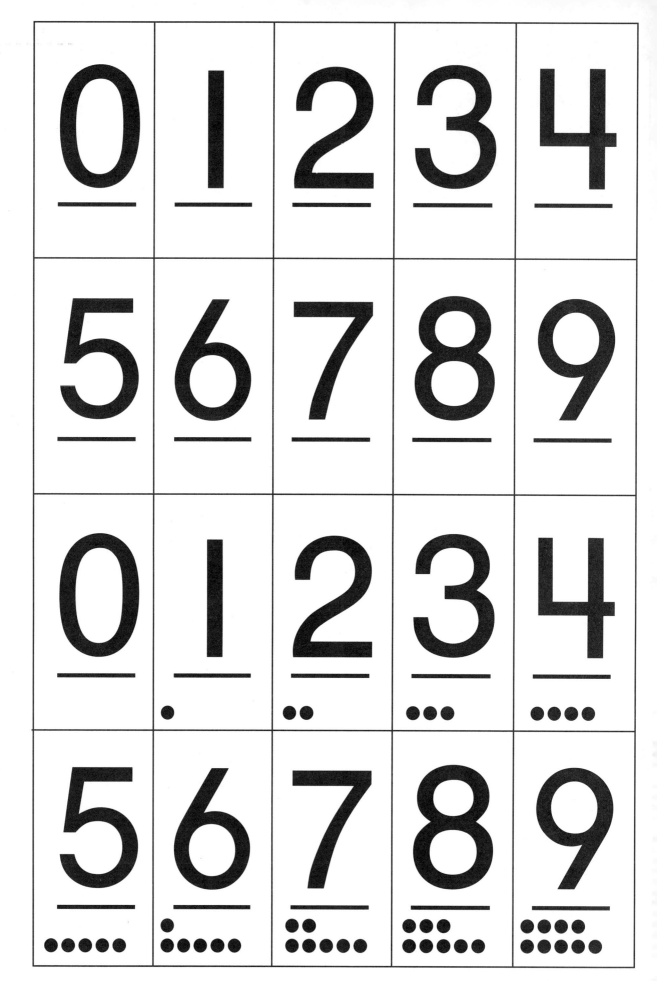

Copyright © Great Source Education Group. All F

5 Domino Blanks

Copyright © Great Source Education Group. All Rights Reserved.

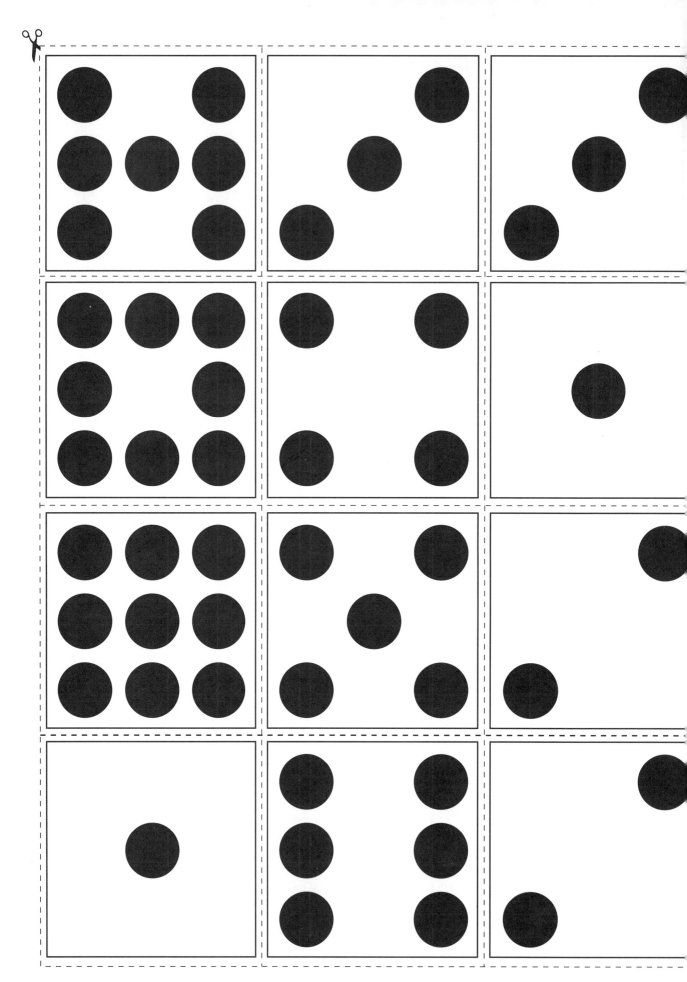

TR6 Domino Halves

Copyright © Great Source Education Group. All Rights Res

Totally Ten Grids

Copyright © Great Source Education Group. All Rights Reserved.

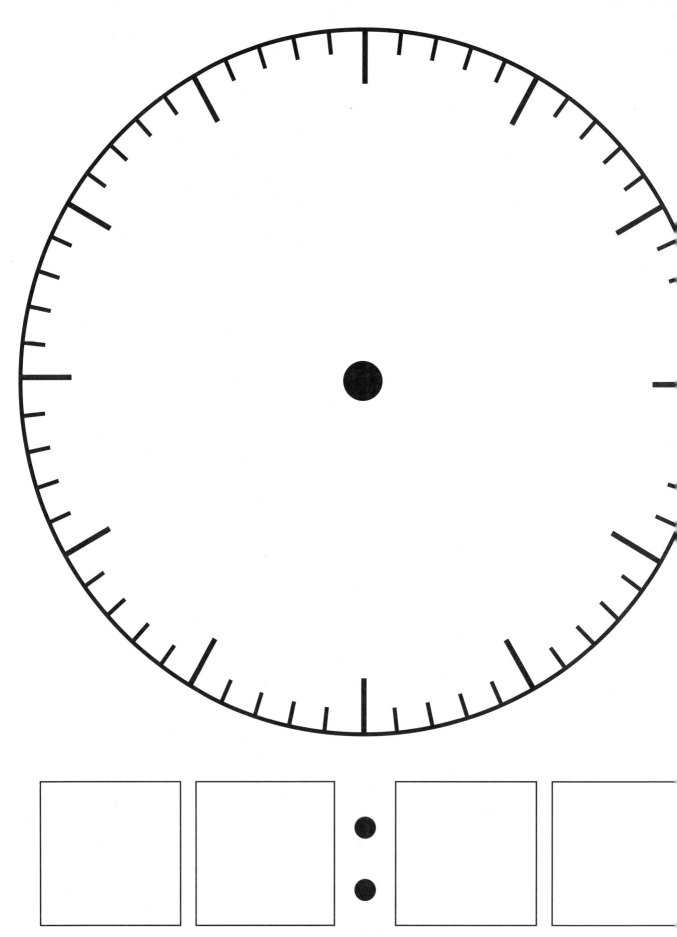

TR8 Every Day Clock

Copyright © Great Source Education Group. All Rights Res

Every Day Graph

Copyright © Great Source Education Group. All Rights Reserved.

Copyright © Great Source Education Group. All Rights Rese

Copyright © Great Source Education Group. All Rights Reserved.

TR12 Weather/Shoe Markers

Copyright © Great Source Education Group. All Rights Reserved

Copyright © Great Source Education Group. All Rights Reserved.

Copyright © Great Source Education Group. All Rights Rese

month _____

Sunday	Monday	Tuesday	Wednesday	Thursday	Friday	Saturday

R15   Calendar Record

Copyright © Great Source Education Group. All Rights Reserved.

1	2	3	4	5	6	7	8	9	10
11	12	13	14	15	16	17	18	19	20
21	22	23	24	25	26	27	28	29	30
31	32	33	34	35	36	37	38	39	40
41	42	43	44	45	46	47	48	49	50
51	52	53	54	55	56	57	58	59	60
61	62	63	64	65	66	67	68	69	70
71	72	73	74	75	76	77	78	79	80
81	82	83	84	85	86	87	88	89	90
91	92	93	94	95	96	97	98	99	100

TR16   Hundred Chart

Copyright © Great Source Education Group. All Rights Reserv

 Copyright © Great Source Education Group. All Rights Reserved.

TR18   Demo Coins: Quarter and Dime, Tails

Copyright © Great Source Education Group. All Rights Reserv

Demo Coins: Nickel and Penny, Heads Copyright © Great Source Education Group. All Rights Reserved.

TR20 **Demo Coins: Nickel and Penny, Tails**

Copyright © Great Source Education Group. All Rights Reserve

yesterday

today

tomorrow

Copyright © Great Source Education Group. All Rights Reserved.

TR22 Calendar Cutouts

Copyright © Great Source Education Group. All Rights Reserv

Blank Hundred Chart

Copyright © Great Source Education Group. All Rights Reserved.

TR24 Coin Comparing Cards

Copyright © Great Source Education Group. All Rights Reserv

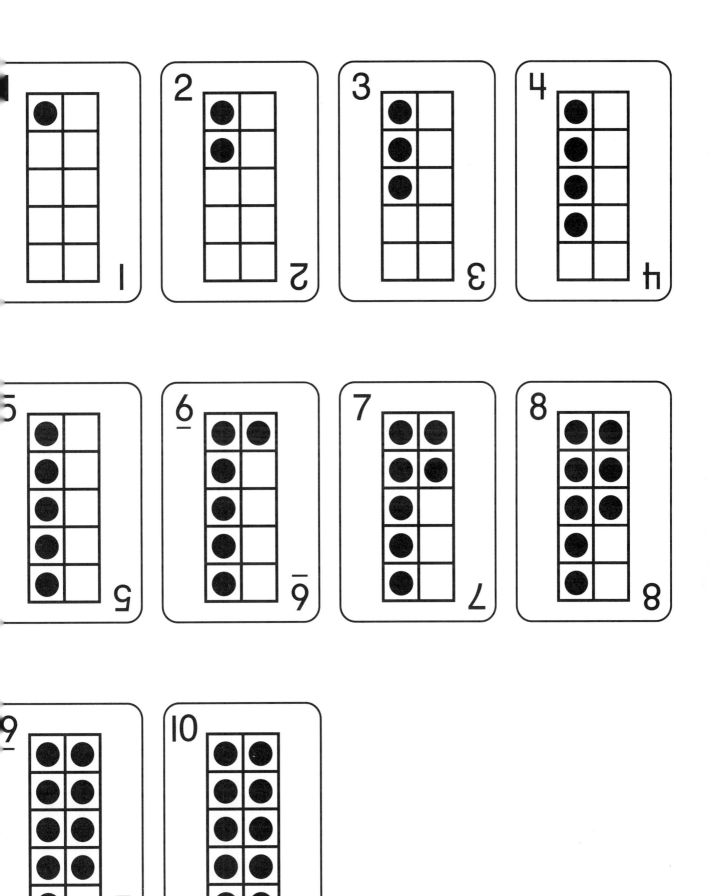

Ten Grid Number Cards

Copyright © Great Source Education Group. All Rights Reserved.

TR26 Centimeter Squared Paper

Copyright © Great Source Education Group. All Rights Reser

Pattern Block Rhombuses/Triangles Copyright © Great Source Education Group. All Rights Reserved.

TR28 Pattern Block Hexagons/Trapezoids

Copyright © Great Source Education Group. All Rights Reser

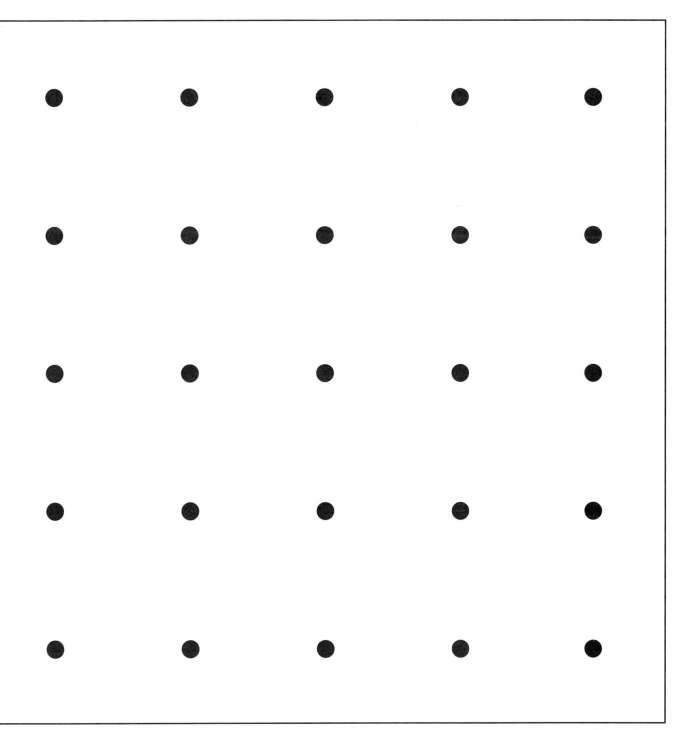

Copyright © Great Source Education Group. All Rights Reserved.

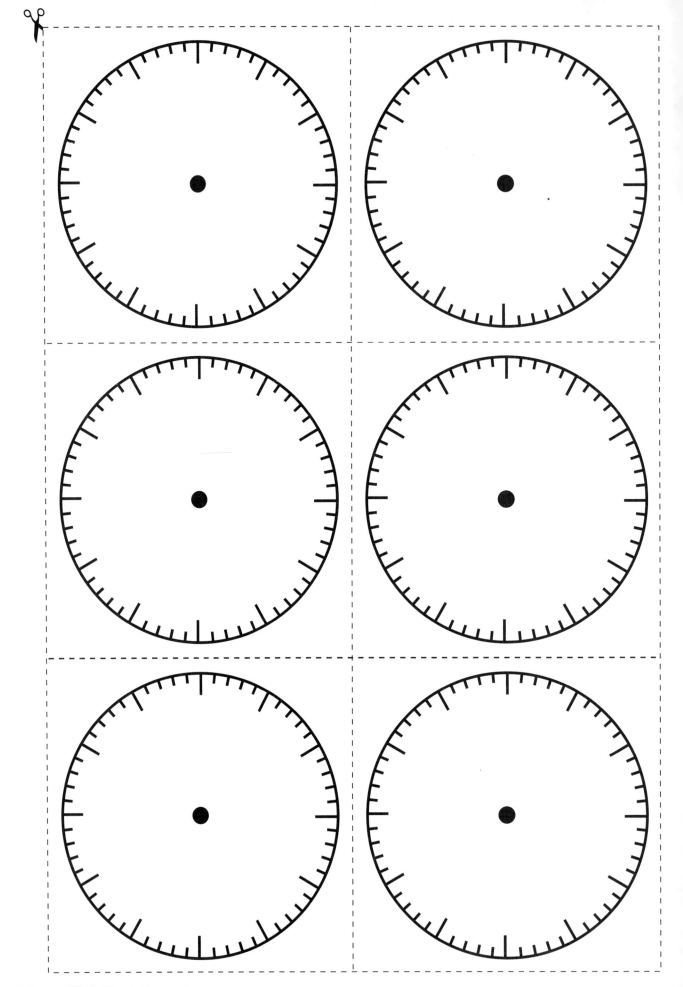

TR30 Mini Clock Records

Copyright © Great Source Education Group. All Rights Rese

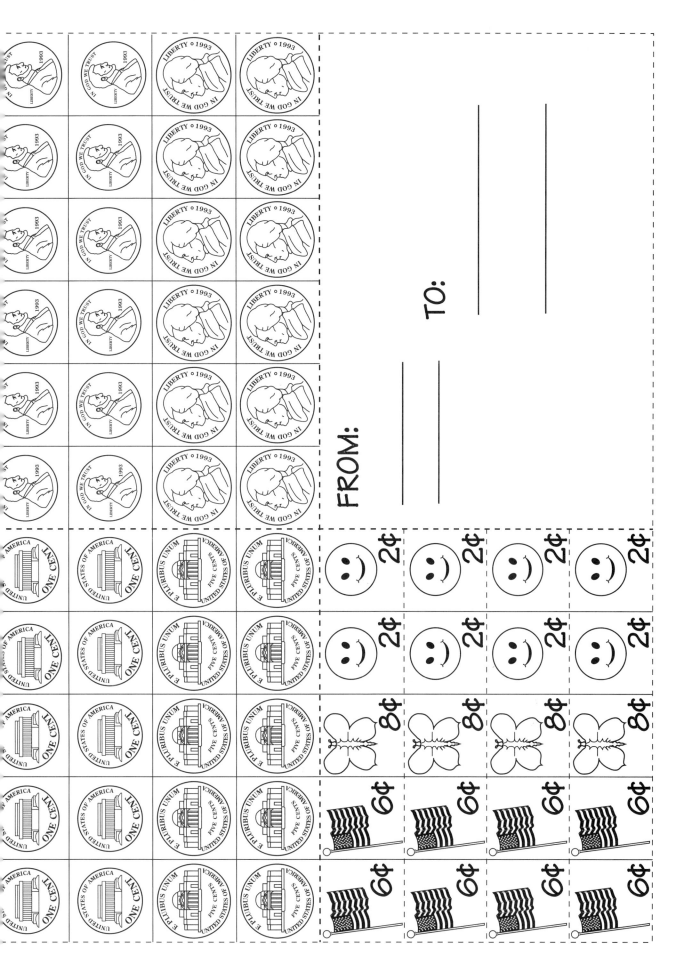

FROM:

TO:

Copyright © Great Source Education Group. All Rights Reserved.